D0916348

THE FRONT COVER

In 1945, Atomic bombs caused World War II to end. After that, the Cold War began. In that era, it was known that dangerous levels of light, heat and radioactivity were prevalent during an atomic bomb attack. All precautions were imposed.

In 1953, When USS Yorktown sailors worked on the weather decks, steel helmets were required along with life jackets, long sleeves rolled down and trouser bottoms tucked into socks, to minimize the effect of an atomic attack.

The location of the author was aft of the island on the catwalk beside the flight deck. The motion picture camera was a 16mm Cine-Kodak Special. Black and white film was used. The film would be processed in the Photo Lab with K3A machines.

This photograph of President John F. Kennedy is exceedingly rare.
Before now, it has never been published.

Most of the photographs in UNDER A HELMET, BEHIND A CAMERA are one of a kind and never before published. This photograph of President John F. Kennedy is exceedingly rare. It was taken aboard one of our submarines on April 14, 1962 by my friend, Chief Photographers Mate Bruce L. Bennett (Deceased). There were a series of photographs taken on that day, this is the only photo that was not turned in. Before now, it has never been published. Chief Bennett gave the only print of it to me! This page is dedicated in memory of my buddy, U.S. Navy Chief Bruce L. Bennett.

UNDER A HELMET, BEHIND A CAMERA

BY

RICHARD G. WELLS

Other books:
A BOY FROM BROWNSVILLE
OVER THE SIDE

INTRODUCTION

1931 was an interesting year. The greatest depression the United States had ever known had dragged it down to the depths of financial ruin.

Al Capone ruled Chicago, Bonnie and Clyde were robbing banks, Prohibition was the Law of the Land and World War II was brewing.

President to be, Franklin D. Roosevelt was outlining the NEW DEAL.

SUPERMAN and Richard Wells were both born in 1931.

Everything was world news, except the arrival of baby Richard Wells, born in Brownsville, Pennsylvania. Like most babies, he didn't know of nor cared about those important times. He was only concerned about eating, sleeping and pooping.

As he grew older, he developed a severe speech problem (Stuttering and blocking.) which made school difficult. But, he had dreams. He wanted to FLY and loved photography! With these in mind, he painfully worked his way through the Brownsville school system and was attending California State Teachers college (In California, Pennsylvania.) when the Korean War broke out.

When the many returning veterans from WWII told stories of their exploits, Richard listened and learned that many things were possible in the military. He enlisted in the US Navy in August 1950. After US Navy Photo School in Pensacola, Florida and a stint at Naval Air Station Memphis, Tennessee, he was assigned to the aircraft carrier USS YORKTOWN CVA 10 in Korean War zone. After four years in the Navy, Richard enlisted in the US Marines for three more years.

This book is one of three books about Richard's life. A BOY FROM BROWNSVILLE and OVER THE SIDE have been successful. This book is about flying, photography and things sea faring men enjoy, but it's mostly about how a stuttering boy from the hills led an exciting life!

PREFACE

This book is different.

Most books about the military tell how many miles they advanced, how many munitions were expended or how a mission was accomplished. UNDER A HELMET, BEHIND A CAMERA does not.

This book is a look at mostly about enlisted men in the United States Navy and the United States Marine Corps. How they live, talk, work and spend their time off duty. Every one had a dedication to duty.

Most of the stories are from recollection of events almost sixty years, before they are put down on paper. Time has an odd way of affecting memory. The bad things dim with time. The fun times stay in the memory to be told time and time again with friends who "have been there", usually around a kitchen table with a cup of coffee.

The stories are brought back to mind through a large collection of photographs that have survived over a half century. With the new electronics, old shipmates can be found and stories retold and verified. It is a big pleasure to find that a liberty buddy of your past is still alive and remembers the exploits. Some of these stories were related to me by people who also "...been there, done that..."

Of course, there are times that are not good to recall. They happened and some will be brought up. Discretion must always be in mind when telling these tales of yore.

When you read this unusual book, imagine what else may have happened. Use your imagination. Look for hidden humor. Most of all, enjoy these sea stories of the WWII, Korean Conflict and the Vietnam experience. (Tales of both at home and abroad.)

The photography and writing of my husband, Richard Wells, has been published in over 80 countries and his photographs of vistas and animals have been used by several artists who have included them in many different art forms such as paintings of the Southwest, Wildlife magazines, calendars and the 1997-8 Florida Duck Stamp.

Richard is a Certified Photographic Consultant, Photo Finishing Engineer, graduate of the US Navy Schools of Photography and Aerial Photography at Pensacola, Florida.

He has won many First Place ribbons, teaches photography in the local school systems and belongs to several nationwide photographic organizations.

While his work takes us many places, we always find interesting local people to meet and listen to-their stories. Sometimes the conversations send us to out-of-the-way photo opportunities.

Our latest trip involved Richard being in an enclosure with a Black Leopard when it charged a six year old boy.

The first night we met, he said, "Life around Richard Wells is never dull!" This has been proved many times over.

- Charlotte A. Wells

Life without risk, challenge, independence
and passion is far more destructive
than physical danger.

- Captain Linda Greenlaw, US Navy

DEDICATION

To my beautiful and loving wife
Charlotte Ann.
Without her love, guidance and red marking pen,
this would never have been written.

It is also dedicated to my four children
Stephen Wells (deceased)
Sandra Jo Hook
Nick Wells (deceased)
Jeffrey Wells, Chief, US Navy (Ret)

And to my four grandchildren
Alden Hook
Austin Hook
Megan Wells
Sydney Wells

UNDER A HELMET, BEHIND A CAMERA
TABLE OF CONTENTS

The author holding a K20 aerial camera.

12

MY FIGHTER PLANE!

World War II had many events that interested me. My greatest desire was to fly. This was enhanced during the Sixth Grade at Prospect Street Elementary School. My efforts as a ten year old boy, to build rubber band powered model airplanes were in vain. Cutting all those little balsa wood strips to assemble the ribs was just too boring. I wanted to FLY! Sitting around, building models was not something I wanted. My desire was to contribute something and be involved as an aviator.

At the time, our elementary school wanted to put on a play to kick off an annual War Bond Drive. The school building was constructed similar to a big, old home with the front entrance that led to a wide staircase. Half way up to the second floor, there was a landing, with another two smaller staircases, one on either side of the landing that led to the second floor.

The students who were not in the play would stand below, at the bottom of the steps. Only actors would perform on the landing. Music would be provided by Mrs. Keys (Our music teacher.) playing the piano.

At that time in my life, I stuttered so badly that being an actor with a speaking part was totally out of the question. But, I volunteered to help in any way I could, never dreaming I could be a real actor.

While other volunteers were selected to impersonate Marines, Sailors and nurses, I thought my job would be a stagehand. Other students who were involved were Ed. Miske, Bill Valsco and Norma Jean Marcolini. Surprisingly, one of the Student Teachers asked me if I would like to play the Army Air Corps Pilot! I couldn't say yes fast enough!

I was able to take a part in the play without being required to speak because a Moderator who would describe what was happening!

I had happily volunteered to be the Army pilot. When my parents would buy hats for me, I would insist on the aviator styled caps, complete with goggles. My helmet, with a short brown jacket, knickers with my favorite knee high, laced up boots almost completed the costume. All I needed was a pair of metal aviator's wings.

The young lady Student Teacher had a boyfriend who was just awarded his silver Army Air Corps pilots wings. He gave them to her. She suggested I wear them in his honor.

Usually, I took very good care of my clothes and hated to punch holes in my leather jacket, even for the wings, but this event was really special for me. The holes would be explainable to my inquisitive mother.

The play went well. As I stepped onto the platform the Army Air Corps Song "Off We Go into the Wild Blue Yonder…." was played by Mrs. Keys. The Moderator referred to me as the Army Air Corps Pilot. You cannot imagine how PROUD I felt!

After the play was over, the rest of the day I strutted about my classes with pride. The bright and gleaming pilot wings attracted a lot of attention from the other students.

The next day, Mother brought home a box of breakfast cereal that had information on the back of the container that attracted my immediate interest. It advertised a cardboard mock up of an airplane cockpit that could be obtained by sending in the box top and a dollar. I begged my Mother to let me have the box top before all of the cereal was eaten. She agreed if only I made sure I ate the rest of the contents.

Next, I needed a dollar. Back in 1940, one dollar was worth a lot more than it is now. I just had to get one, plus a stamp and envelope.

I talked to my Dad and made a bargain with him. He said I would have to tend the furnace for a month for the dollar. This meant I would need to keep the fire going by shoveling in coal, removing and carrying out ashes. I quickly

Piper Cub J-3

Grumman F4F-3

agreed.

Mother would furnish the envelope and stamp.

After putting the box top and the dollar in the addressed envelope and depositing it at the post office. I began to wait and wait and wait.

After two weeks of waiting, a very large brown envelope was delivered by Mr. Mossit, the mailman. ! I couldn't wait to open it. It included a folded cardboard cockpit of a Piper J -3 airplane. The instructions were to place the unfolded cockpit on a low surface, like a card table. As I opened it up, it showed a turn and bank indicator, airspeed indicator, altimeter, compass and an engine revolution per minute indicator. I had seen instruments like these on airplane instrument panels in the wartime movies about flying.

Of course, none of these actually worked, they were part of the paper that was adhered to the cardboard. They appeared to be quite authentic looking to me.

My control stick was unfolded with the attached cardboard on the floor with the foot pedals. I stood up the cardboard control panel on its bottom edge and properly arranged the other components. I was finally ready to fly!

After hurriedly putting on my helmet, jacket, knickers and boots, I carefully studied the booklet of How to Fly. The little book said it was a true –to- life mock up of a J-3 Piper Cub. But in my imagination, it was a Navy F4F-3 Grumman Fighter Plane.

My past reading included information about the F4F-3, so to me, it had a tail hook, retractable landing gear complete with manual crank, four fifty caliber machine guns and a 1830-66 Twin Wasp radial engine! (At that time, I knew nothing of landing flaps, trim tabs, rate of climb indicators or any other instruments on a real airplane.)

The information described how to start the aircraft (The J-3 had to be "Pulled through by hand" to get the motor started but the F4F-3 had a self starter.)

I studied how to taxi the plane to the runway, turn it into the wind, lock the brakes, "rev" up the engine, and release the brakes to enable the craft to roll down the runway. As it went faster, the tail would rise from the ground. When the airspeed rose to about 70 knots, the plane would try to become airborne. The book said I must hold it horizontal until adequate airspeed was obtained by keeping the tail up and the nose down. Then, gently pull back on the stick. The little Cub gently rose. But, my imaginary Grumman with the big three bladed propeller would streak skyward like a homesick angel!

After being airborne, I would crank the landing gear up and into the fuselage. Of course, the little J-3 Cub did not have retractable gear but my imaginary F4F-3 retracted them into the fuselage right below and forward of, the wing roots.

Then I would give it full throttle, pull the stick back to hang the Grumman on its big three bladed propeller and zoom straight up! I would imagine my speedy and quick fighter was yanked up by its propeller, screaming upward, through the clouds up into the clear blue sunny skies. The roar and vibrations of the vertical ascent was exciting.

The F4F-3 responded quite well. I practiced inside and outside loops, Immelman turns, hammerhead stalls and perfected my inverted flight by using the control stick and rudder pedals as the instruction book directed. Quickly, I was confident enough to believe I could survive an aerial dogfight. I was READY!

Every night, after doing my homework, my imaginary Navy F4F-3 fighter plane and I would fly mission after mission, dropping bombs on enemy targets and engaging Japanese Zero fighter planes in mortal combat.

Sometimes, my vocal sounds of the big, roaring radial engine of my powerful craft and the rattle of its four fifty caliber machine guns would disturb my Father while he was trying to read the Brownsville Telegraph. He didn't like war or the playing of war but because he knew I loved to fly, his complaints were few and far between.

After awhile, I just KNEW I could fly an airplane if I had the chance. Little did I dream that someday I would be at the controls of real Navy planes such as SNJ's, JRB's, PB4Y2's and the beautiful PBY-5 Catalina Flying Boats.

After enlisting in the US Navy during the Korean War years, I managed to get into the Navy Air Wing as an Aerial Photographer/Combat Aircrewman. Best of all, on long tiring flights, the pilots would permit me to actually fly the planes. Of course, they would be in intercom contact with me if I would have needed them.

The US Navy enabled my dreams to come true!

US ARMY ASSAULT

In the summer of 1942, my Dad came home from work with a small brown envelope. He came to me and said, "Richie, I have a surprise for you!" There were two tickets in the envelope.

"You and I will be going to Forbes Field (The predecessor of Three Rivers Stadium) in Pittsburgh! You will enjoy this. Just you and I!

Because he did not tell me what the event was all about, until the next Saturday when we were to take the long, rare, curvy trip to Pittsburgh, I was not only curious but also excited. Imagine, just Dad and I will be going to Pittsburgh!

On the appointed day, we got into the old 1933 Chevy and navigated the 35 miles to Forbes Stadium. As we went to our seats, I saw a big sign with pictures of army tanks, soldiers with guns and drawings of explosions! By this time, I knew we were not there to see a baseball game! But, WHAT are we here FOR? And, what was on the other end of the grassy field? It appeared to be camouflage netting!

Then, all at once, there were very loud noises coming from the netting on the other end of the arena!

At first, it startled everybody in the stadium, but it seemed that everyone else knew what was going on but ME! I asked, "DAD! WHAT did you bring me to?"

POW! BANG! POW! CRASH! BANG! POW! POW!

The assault began with cannon fire from hidden positions. The guns were unseen, but the cordite in the smoke from the gunfire was pungent.

If you looked sharply enough, you could see some large dark objects slowly moving on the other side of the field of battle. They were tanks with the accompanying infantry. They moved slowly, tanks drew fire, which infantry does not appreciate but the tanks needed the infantry to protect the big, steel, green behemoths from being overrun by opposing infantry, possibly with flame throwers, rockets or Molotov Cocktails. The tanks and the infantry depended upon each other.

It was terrifying to see and horrifying to realize the force and power behind the assault. From my place, not only were the aggressors in sight but I knew the defenders were well hidden and would defend their positions as well as possible.

The crackle of small arms fire, rifles, pistols and light machine guns began. At first it sounded like firecrackers but when the steady, regular fire of the automatic weapons began, you knew it was a determined fight.

The tank's guns increasing the roar while spitting fire and smoke with their slow heavy cannons toward the defenders emplacements. When they moved to be in sight of the enemy, counter fire began. First the small arms and then bigger guns and mortars added to the firefight. The noise was deafening. Night was falling and the sparkling lights of the small arms and the bigger flashes of the cannons lit up the field. Men in the open began to drop. At first it was one at a time, and then as they got closer to the defenders hidden emplacements, the aggressors dropped more often. It was impossible to tell how many men were being lost.

The night sky was being lit up. The noise was overwhelming. I was safe, but watching the scene scared me. These were all new sights for me. Never before in my life had I witnessed the ferocity of a combat situation. Not only the constant small arms fire, but the screaming of the men, the powerful tank engines roaring, all with the crew manned weapons noises. The Combat Medics were administering first aid when it could help the downed men. It was just too much to experience the horrors of war, right before my eyes.

Even though it was a warm night, what I witnessed made me sweaty, cold and trembling with fear because of my compassion for the troops.

I moved a bit closer to my Dad. He understood.

Dad was a Coal Mining Foreman at Clyde #3 mine in Clarksville, Pa. The Company was participating in a Nationwide War Bond Drive. If an employee bought a $100 dollar War Bond (Cost of the bond was $75.00), two tickets to the war game would be given to the purchaser. It was widely touted as being close to the "real thing". It was. It taught this little boy very much. I learned many things that night. Most of all, to stay out of tank and infantry warfare and to really respect what our military men were doing for our Country, fighting and dying.

The main point of this spectacle was not only to give something back to the many people who bought War Bonds but to show them what their money was doing. It was helping us win World War II.

There were people in the audience who screamed and cried. Some, while trying to hide the tears or disgust, left the show before it was over.

(A similar circumstance was depicted in the book and the movie, FLAGS OF OUR FATHERS.)

After that experience, never again did I hear about those shows. It is possible it came too close to the feelings of so many people that it was counter productive to the War Bond efforts.

At that time, we were losing almost 400 young men every hour of the day. The war games were too "close to home."

While on the long, dark ride home, Dad was unusually quiet. Never again would he permit me to play war in his presence.

JOHN R. LAMONICA, US ARMY COMBAT MEDIC

As the LCVP's (Landing Craft, Vehicles or Personnel) sped toward the white sand beach of Oran, North Africa, my Uncle, US Army Combat Medic John R. LaMonica was worried. He clutched his medical bag tightly. He prayed his bloody work that was ahead would help save lives. This was his first landing on a hostile beachhead. Crowded in the flat bottomed boat were other apprehensive soldiers. The Sergeant told them, "If you ain't scared, you ain't human!"

The bow of the craft slid close to the sandy beach. The ramp dropped with a rattle and a splash. The moment they all feared had arrived. At that point in time, all the troops pray there is no machine gun pointed at the new opening in the bow. The guys stomped forward and jumped into the foot deep surf, hoping not to step into a water covered, shell hole. With a few running steps they reached the tall grass that lined the beach. Surprising, there was not much incoming fire from the French who the Germans were expecting to stop the Allied invasion. The generals who planned the landing anticipated much more resistance. The landing was deemed successful.

Uncle Johnnie was born and raised in the village of New Boro in Southwest Pennsylvania. While growing up, he helped his family of 12 children operate the family business, a greenhouse. His parents had emigrated from Sicily. There was not any real entertainment in those days. Survival meant working, 24 hours per day, seven days a week. When Johnnie did sneak some spare time, he would go to the nearest village and gamble. There, he found games of penny tossing, dice and cards right on the sidewalks of the little coal mining village. As Johnnie grew, so did his proficiency in games of skill and chance.

When the Japanese bombed Pearl Harbor on December 7, 1941, it was on John's birthday; he took it personal. He enlisted and on January 15, 1942 he left home for the US ARMY. After his recruit training, he was sent to Combat Medic School for 8 weeks. Johnnie found this appealing. He wouldn't be carrying a weapon and instead, would be helping people. This fit in with his personality.

Johnnie's big smile and genial ways made friends with everyone he met. His Sicilian charm worked well for him. When he won at cards, the other players rarely minded. He actually made them feel (almost) good about it.

(I speak firsthand about the feelings. Every Christmas at my Grandparent's house, there would be an Italian card game with the whole family. The game was called Seven and a Half. (Sette-e-Messo, in Italian.) It was similar to Blackjack but with a lower goal. John was very good at taking the pennies from all of us kids with a big smile and a joke. It was all in good natured fun, even though; we kids hated losing our few pennies. He ALWAYS keeps his winnings!)

In the Army, playing cards and shooting craps was a natural pastime for Johnnie. He loved the games and was very good at them. Most of the new soldiers weren't clever enough to keep up with Johnnie.

When there was a job to do, Johnnie did it well and with a big smile and a wisecrack to keep the mood as cheerful as possible. He made many friends in the army, while relieving them of their money and other valuables.

After the initial landing, he tended to the wounded, worked as a stretcher bearer and performed other tasks as assigned to him. Once, while on a train transporting wounded soldiers to a hospital near Oran, the train was stopped near an orange grove. The troops hadn't seen fresh oranges for months. Against direct orders, Johnnie jumped off the train, ran into the grove, opened his shirt collar buttons and stuffed as many ripe, juicy oranges into his shirt as possible. He then ran back to the train with his overloaded shirt and climbed back aboard. He distributed the ill gotten treasure among the wounded troops. He was that kind of a guy.

After the North African fighting ended, he was with the first wave of American troops landing on Sicily. Our family had emigrated from Sicily and he had relatives still living there. He unsuccessfully tried to contact them. Due to the pressures of the conflict, he was not able to look for them. He always regretted that but he had a job to do and would not venture off on a personal mission.

The fighting through Sicily and crossing the Straights of Messina brought him into Italy. During the battles with the Germans, he was included in the bloody, inept, poorly planned landing at the Anzio/Salerno Beachhead. He was then assigned to the US Army Hospital Ship USAHS ARCADIA. The ship was taking the wounded from the bloody battlefield to hospitals in England.

For the three years prior to this, America didn't have any hospital ships. There was a very long discussion in the United States Congress as to who would control the hospital ships. Both the Army and the Navy wanted to be in charge of them. Finally, it was resolved that the Navy would operate the ships and the Army would attend the wounded. The first hospital ships were sent to the European theater of war.

PFC LaMonica was glad to be assigned to the USAHS ARCADIA. This ship was painted completely white with a large comforting red cross on the side of the hull. The sides of the ship were brightly lit at night. The Geneva Convention required hospital shops not to carry fresh troops, guns or ammunitions.

The USAHS Arcadia was manned by the US Navy and staffed a US Army medical complement of 12 officers, 1 Warrant officer, 35 nurses and 99 enlisted men. They would care for 500 patients. However, in time of need, supplementary units could be added. Each supplementary unit consisted of 2 officers, 4 nurses and 11 enlisted men for every 100 additional patients.

Early one evening, while plying the dangerous waters of the Mediterranean Sea, steaming toward Gibraltar, a German submarine surfaced to hail the hospital ship, demanding it stop for inspection. Combatants had the Geneva Convention right to stop hospital ships to determine if they were transporting anything except wounded soldiers.

The ship was stopped dead in the water. The Germans boarded the ship and began their inspection. While doing that, a German officer mentioned, "We

USAHS ARCADIA, in Southhampton, England off-loading wounded.

John with a family he befriended in Naples, Italy.

25

have a crewman aboard our vessel that needs medical attention, would you be so kind as to help him?" Naturally, it was agreed to attend to the man's needs.

The stricken submariner was brought aboard and was attended to by the American doctors. Because this happened around mealtime, the German officers were asked if they wished to dine with the ship's officers. They gladly accepted.

After the Germans were satisfied that there were no contraband aboard the USAHS ARCADIA, they returned their crewman to the U Boat, saluted the big white ship and both sailed apart. That night, many aboard the illuminated ship had their private thoughts. Some imagined submarines torpedoing the ship, others of airplanes bombing and if sometimes, if they were wounded would the Germans doctors aid them as we Americans did theirs?

As the USAHS ARCADIA steamed toward England to pick up more wounded, PFC LaMonica received a letter from his sister Victoria. She had married a Sgt. Ivan Buchanan who was a M 4 Tank commander with General Patton. Ivan's leg was badly wounded near Bastogne and he was in a hospital at Portsmouth, England. Ivan had written to his wife Vicki, that the American doctors wanted to amputate the leg, but in a newly captured German hospital, a German Surgeon Colonel did emergency surgery and saved his leg.

As soon as the ship docked, Johnnie, with Ivan's letter in hand, went directly to the hospital, found which ward and bed Sgt. Buchanan was located. Johnnie walked up to Ivan and said, "Ivan, I am your wife Vick's brother John. I am your new Brother in Law!" They had a great visit until "lights out!" and Johnnie had to return to his ship.

Medic LaMonica was then transferred to a different type of hospital ship. The new ships were actually pre war high speed ocean liners. These ships had been converted to the hospital ship duties because of their ability to outrun submarines or surface vessels. The plush interiors had been removed and replaced with military style steel bunks, cabinets, operating rooms and dining areas. Best of all, there were many spaces where a bit of card playing or

Hospital ship personel.

shooting craps could take place. (Johnnie never said it was the famous HMS QUEEN MARY, but once, hinted it was.) Johnnie used to brag, "I've crossed the ocean more times than most sailors!"

Those ships were camouflage painted and no marking to conform to the Geneva Conventions. After unloading the wounded men in the U.S.A., on the return trip they probably carried war material across the Atlantic to the European Theater of War.

John enjoyed this duty. He could complete his duties as a Medic then gamble in his time off. He was very good at remembering the cards being played, what the odds were and how to efficiently wager. He acquired many war items such as German flags, pistols, medals, daggers and other war trophies. He would sell them to the sailors. Of course, he won a lot of money, too!

One of the times, when his ship was in New York Harbor for a week, he came home for a few days. He brought a big sack full of green boxes of toy army trucks, jeeps and tanks. He gave one box to his little brother Jerry, nephews Eddie Rabbitts and me. We were jumping up and down in anticipation of which truck or other vehicle we might get from our Wonderful Uncle Johnnie who thought of US!

When World War II was over, Johnnie was discharged on December 16, 1945 with the rank of Tec 5.

John became a florist, married beautiful Betty Lichney, raised Arabian horses and lived happily ever after.

My Uncle Johnnie recieved what he deserved for the good work he had done as a US Army Combat Medic. Hopefully, this story will be a remembrance of him and of others like him who faithfully served OUR Country when they were needed.

Medic John R. LaMonica

*John and his bride, Betty Lichney of
near Republic, PA.*

John helping to feed North African kids.

SMALLTOWN, U.S.A. DURING WW II

In the typical small town of Brownsville, Pa., where I was growing up during WWII, living was much different than it was before the war.

After the war began, there were many jobs to be had. High paying jobs in the coal mines, boat building, on the railroads and in the alcohol industry. Most people were making alot of money.

One of the lucrative occupations was the printing and selling of counterfeit Ration Cards and Stamps. You needed Government issued stamps for gasoline, food, shoes, tires and other vital items that were also needed for the war effort.

The War Effort even affected cigarettes. They were hard to find and prices skyrocketed to almost FIFTY CENTS A PACK! Lucky Strike cigarettes came in a green pack. The government needed green paint for tanks, trucks and Jeeps. Lucky Strike adapted by making the green part of the pack white, which needed no color at all. They used the saying, "LUCKY STRIKE GREEN HAS GONE TO WAR!" Naturally, the change reduced the cost of the packaging. But not the price!

The war effort needed steel. Coal and coke were needed to fuel the blast furnaces at the Pittsburgh steel mills. (Coke is to coal as charcoal is to wood.) Coal mining was hard, dirty work for the men but the burning of the coke ovens made the sky black. In addition to the coke ovens, there were mountains of the unusable slate mixed with coal outside every coal mine. These were usually burning day and night and emitted more dense black smoke and sulphuric gas.

When visiting relations in Allison, one night when the ovens were burning, I sat on the front porch and read a newspaper.

The Southwest Pennsylvania mining area was an unsafe place to live. Every day, many people died from consumption and various forms of cancer as a

Typical small town of Brownsville, PA.

result of the noxious smoke and fumes from the coal mining industry.

Our men and boys were being drafted into the military and sent to far off places we had never heard of, some in the USA but most went overseas. At first, we did not realize the toll of the men we had sent, later it became too obvious.

We all had friends, relations and neighbors who had answered the call to the service of our Country. The results of this began to trickle in to us by the newspapers and MOVIETONE NEWS when we would go to the motion picture theaters.

We knew most of our boys were being trained to fight. Some of them were in the Navy aboard ships plying the cold North Atlantic while trying to protect the merchant ships that were taking war material to Russia and England on the LEND LEASE arrangements. The German submarine packs were taking a terrible toll. Looking seaward from our Nation's shores at night, you could see burning ships.

One of our neighbors, Glen Swogger, was a merchant marine sailor. Three ships were torpedoed from under him. One of these ships was sunk right after it saved him from another sinking ship in the frigid, dangerous water of the North Atlantic.

When our military began to take the offensive, the tragic battle tolls began to come into our little river town. They began to add up. A death here and there and the wounded began to trickle home. Most of the returnees did not talk about their experiences. When some did, it was pure horror. As these stories began to be passed around the little town, we became more aware of what our young boys were being subjected to in far off places.

All gave some, some gave all.

When the telegraph boy would deliver the fateful telegram that began, "We regret to inform you….." it would be terrible for the family and close friends. Most just couldn't believe their young son was gone from them….forever.

Many screams, hair pulling and panic would strike mothers and fathers alike. Most of the dead would be buried where they died.

The unthinkable amount of losses was not told to the civilians. The actual amounts were almost FOUR HUNDRED DEAD EVERY HOUR OF EVERY DAY, SEVEN DAYS A WEEK!

The losses of the air crews over Europe, the Marines in the Pacific, the sailors of sea battles, soldiers dying in the mud and many other instances of terror kept the losses at unimaginable totals.

All the information we civilians received was the good news or what had been slanted to hide the truth from us.

On June 6, 1944, D DAY at Normandy, France was particularly terrible. Several men from Brownsville were there. Two of them were brothers. They were about a mile apart that day. On the second day, one of the brothers went to try to find his brother. When he found the Company his brother served with, they told the man his brother was killed the day before.

When Jimmy Dolittle led the first bombing raid on Japan, the flyers that were captured were declared "war criminals" by the Japanese. They were beheaded with samurai swords and their stripped bodies fed to the animals in the Tokyo Zoo. That was captured on Japanese film that was shown in the local theaters.

There were too many stories to relate, but when all this filtered down to our little town of about 3,500 persons, we were all dismayed and more determined to do everything to win the war.

When there were scrap drives, we saved aluminum for the drive. It seemed we found the metal everywhere. Even a rolled up aluminum toothpaste tube was valuable. Every housewife donated left over cooking grease and extra pots and pans; even the WWI and Civil War cannons that decorated the schools and parks were donated. Taking pleasure auto trips was not done. Gasoline, oil, tires and batteries were all scarce and rationed. Families who lived along railroad tracks would pick up coal that had dropped from the long trains huffing and puffing to the steel mills in Pittsburgh. Some of the trainmen felt sorry for the people who searched the tracks. The trainmen would toss out lumps of coal for them. The people and the railroad men would wave to each other whenever this would happen.

And, of course, everyone who had some extra space planted "VICTORY GARDENS." Much of the garden produce was canned by the wives in Mason Jars. Buying new shoes needed ration stamps, so the shoe repair shops were busy all the time. Automobile and truck tires were always recapped with new tread as many times as possible. Personally, I worked at the Atlantic Gas station in West Brownsville. We recapped tires for cars and big ten ton coal hauling trucks.

Even though it was hard times for the civilian population, we didn't mind because we knew what our boys were doing and they needed our help. Our imaginations told us what would happen to us if we lost the War! We all had read or seen the news reports of the Rape of Nanking, the Bataan Death March, the concentration camps, the deaths at Warsaw. We knew what would happen to us!

Every one pitched in. It was actually a time of National comradeship. We were ALL in the "boat" and did NOT want it to go under!

RATIONING AND WAR BONDS DURING WW II

During the war, all material to aid the war effort was hard to get. This included automobiles, trucks, gasoline, tires, oil, aluminum, radios, tin froil, flour, iron, steel, cigarettes, shoes, meat, photographic supplies, sugar, coffee and food in general.

To keep people from hoarding scarce items, rationing was instituted by the Federal Government. This was done by a government employee deciding how much of what you could have in accordance by who lived at an address. More people in the family, more ration stamps you were allotted. For gasoline, tires and oil, it was determined by what kind of work you did and how far you had to drive to get there. A decal was placed on the windshield of each car or truck designating what group of gasoline stamps you were legally allowed to have.

All ration stamps were not alike. Some were for food or for gasoline and other different stamps for other necessities. Naturally, these stamps were more important than money. You could earn more money but not qualify for more stamps. Of course, that resulted in counterfeiting. It was a Federal Offense to counterfeit ration stamps.

Some controlled items had serial numbers, tires, for example. When you bought a tire, the serial number from the tire was recorded and written on your application to be able to purchase it.

People like my Father, who had an old 1933 Chevrolet, were stuck with them when the war broke out. This was very inconvenient for people who had to drive a long way to work. There were no new cars built during the war years. Replacement parts were scarce, too! Very few people complained about rationing because we all knew it was to help our boys to win the bloody war.

After the war was over, the auto industry began to build cars in 1946. For years after that, a purchaser of a new car had to pay list price plus $100 "under the table" for a new car. In 1948, my Dad bought a brand new 1947

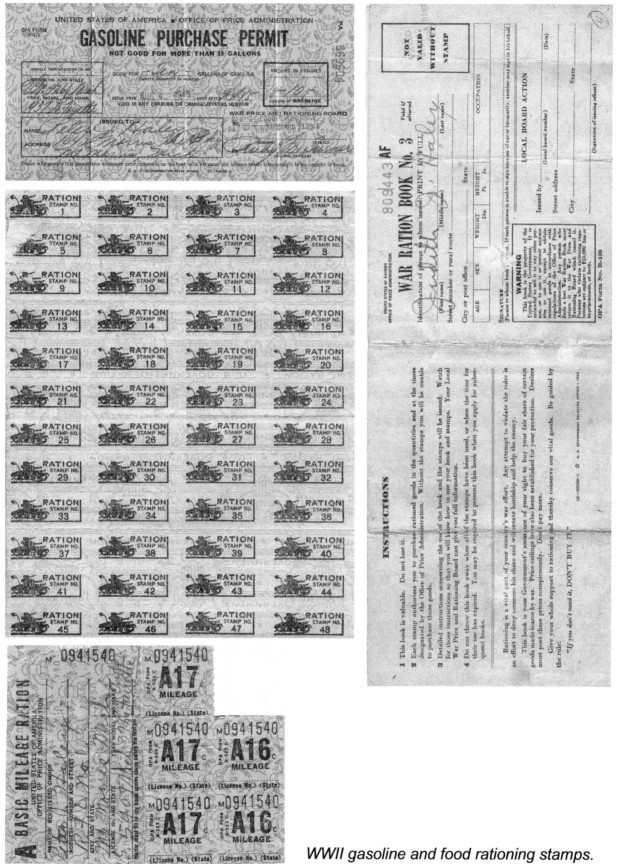

WWII gasoline and food rationing stamps.

Chevy and still had to pay the extra $100.00 over the list price of $1,535 to buy it from the Chevrolet dealer in Fredricktown, Pa.

My best friend, Kenny Rinehart was with me when I wrecked this new car. We had just washed and waxed it and were going to see some girls upriver. We turned left off Rt.40 on to Rt. 88 when an older car in front of us with Ohio license plates abruptly stopped. The people were looking at the river Locks, right across the river. I had been distracted for a moment and when I looked up, the other car was right in front of me. I pushed quickly and firmly on those mechanical brakes. The Chevy would not stop quickly enough. Rather than hitting the rear end of that old car, with people sitting in the back seat, I turned the steering wheel to the left. That directed me into the empty oncoming lane. I skidded across the narrow, two lane road and hit the guard rail. It stopped the new Chevy from going over the bank and down fifty feet onto the Pennsylvania Railroad tracks. The cables between the sturdy posts ripped the shiny new grill and the metal front fender like a can opener. The car came to a stop with the grill wrapped around a six inch diameter wooden guard rail post.

When Dad came to see the car at the Dealership, it was the ONLY time he ever swore at me. He said, "DAMN YOU!" His frustration was because his car was his only way to get to work at the Clyde #3 coal mine at Clarksville, Pa. He was a Boss there and it required him to be there every day. The dealership did a rush job on the car for Dad. He was only off work for one day because of my poor driving.

My maternal Grandfather, Joseph LaMonica, had a partial solution to the problem of food rationing. He owned a greenhouse in New Boro. It had about 20 hotbeds around it. He would plant tomato, pepper and cabbage seeds in these hotbeds. When they grew to seedlings, they were transplanted into low wooden boxes called flats. They were about 12 inches wide, 18 inches long and three inches deep. The soil for these plants was meticulously a mix of black dirt, horse manure and a bit of sand. They would grow to the proper height to plant in gardens. Grandpa, Uncle Charlie and Uncle Johnnie cleaned out coal mines' stables to get the horse manure.

In the area were many coal mines, coke ovens and other industries that employed many immigrants from Eastern and Southern Europe. These people worked hard at their jobs and took great pleasure in building gardens. These customers flocked to the greenhouse. Retail outlets, markets, hardware stores and other places also bought plants for resale. The demand grew so much for the plants that Grampa needed three trucks to deliver them.

The whole family worked together to grow and prepare more and more of these boxed plants. The demand grew to the point where the trucks would also deliver to the company houses of the local coal mines.

Company houses were something like a subdivision built on the company property of the mines. You had to work in that particular mine to rent half of a duplex home. The rent would be automatically deducted from your paycheck. Each group of houses would be called a "patch" and in a central location there would be a Company Store. Purchases would be deducted from your pay. The Company store would also buy plants to resell. Grampa and his family were very busy.

Every summer, I would take a week "vacation" to Grampa and Grammas. There I would help doing what ever Grampa wanted me to do. At eleven or twelve years old, I would work with my Uncle Jerry who was two years younger than I. Grampa had many little jobs for us to learn. The hardest job was for Jerry and me to use a double handled crosscut saw to saw old railroad ties to a proper length to fit in the greenhouse furnace. (The workers on the Pennsylvania Railroad would drop off unusable ties at the greenhouse.)

In addition to the vegetable plants, on Mothers and Fathers days the locals would stop by the greenhouse and purchase carnations to wear. Red ones if the parent was alive and white if they were deceased. Poinsettias were sold around the Christmas season. Flowers like petunias, zinnias and others were sold in the proper seasons. This was a win-win-win situation for Grandpa, the people and the Government.

Our Nation needed MONEY. The War Bond Drives took not only our folding money but our nickels and dimes, too!

School kids were encouraged to buy Savings Stamps for a dime each. They were pasted in little stamp books. When the books were full with $18.75 worth of stamps, we could take them to school and turn them in for a $25.00 war bond. Different classes and schools would compete to decide a winner of who sold the most stamps and bonds. We were very proud when we earned a $25.00 bond that we only paid $18.75 to get! Many War Bond Contest winners were rewarded by a write up and photograph in the local newspaper. Actually, when we were told that we were helping to finance the war to save our future, we believed it because it was the truth!

I shoveled snow, filled coal bins, collected scrap, sold newspapers or anything else to make a bit of money; I would buy stamps with whatever I earned. My parents encouraged this thriftiness.

When I was in the seventh grade, there was a special war bond drive. Our school, Brownsville Junior High, announced that as a special event, the first person who bought a bond during the drive would get their photo and a write up in the Brownsville Telegraph! The Bond Drive began on a cold, snowy

January Monday morning!

I just happened to have a stamp book full. It could buy a $25.00 bond on the first day and I would be the FIRST one in my school to buy one! On that Monday morning, the school would open up at 8am. At 7am, I was at the front door, shivering in the cold, clutching my filled war stamp book in my gloved hand! I would be the FIRST one! My story and picture would be in the BROWNSVILLE TELEGRAPH! My nose was running so much, I filled my only handkerchief and my face, legs and feet felt icy.

As soon as the doors opened, I ran into the school, through the empty halls, down to the door of the classroom of the Art teacher, the elderly Mrs. Eva Williams who was handling the bond drive! She was sitting at her desk!

Mrs. Williams did not immediately realize I was not only very cold but also stuttered badly. With those two situations, she was caught off guard.

I ran up to her, excited, panting and cold and blurted out, "MMMrs. WWWilliams! HHHHERE is my SSSSTamp book! It is ffffull of the sssstamps I have bbbbought from you for the lllast Ssssix months! AAAAM I the fffirst one to buy a bbbond?"

Mrs. Williams showed surprise as her eyes opened wide! Then, as she realized the situation, she slowly closed them, put her head down and softly said, "Richard, you are too late. The principal sold the first one, last night. Sunday night. The reporter and photographer from the Telegraph have already taken the picture and it will be in the paper this afternoon with the story of another student buying the first bond. She is the daughter of "Mr. S......, a local attorney."

I was crestfallen! I was unfairly beaten out of the patriotic effort that I made. Mrs. Williams seemed very sad. She looked down at me, took both of her warm hands, covered my icy ones and softly said, "Richard, I am so sorry. But, it's too late."

When the war ended and it was announced, Brownsville's down town area was full of honking horns, people screaming and a large commotion. We heard it because we lived up the hill. I asked my Mother if I could do downtown. She said "No, you don't know what people will do. It may be dangerous." As the obedient child I was, the afternoon was spent with some wood and a saw, listening to the big party downtown. I made a wooden rifle. In the process, I accidentally cut my left arm with a hand saw. For the past seventy years, I still have the scar on my forearm.

By the time the war was over, I had several bonds that were issued in my name, bought with the money acquired from doing odd jobs. I was proud of each and every one of them!

They represented faith in my Country, a lot of hard work, and great memories. They represented a pride that I had helped win the Second World War in my own small way!

After the war ended, the demand for steel diminished. The coal mines, coke ovens and other businesses closed. Most of the people moved to the cities. The ones who died from coal mining injuries or breathing the chemical laden smoke from the coke ovens are buried in the many simple graveyards. The homes and other buildings that were in the area have been stripped to a few foundations. Green grass and new trees are taking back the land that had been raped to win the war against the Axis powers. Fayette County is now resting among those beautiful, old, green, Appalachian Mountains.

The Monongahela River is not a dirty, chemical laden brown anymore. It is again a beautiful blue!

INSTRUMENT OF SURRENDER

W e, acting by command of and in behalf of the Emperor of Japan, the Japanese Government and the Japanese Imperial General Headquarters, hereby accept the provisions set forth in the declaration issued by the heads of the Governments of the United States, China and Great Britain on 26 July 1945, of Potsdam, and subsequently adhered to by the Union of Soviet Socialist Republics, which four powers are hereafter referred to as the Allied Powers.

We hereby proclaim the unconditional surrender to the Allied Powers of the Japanese Imperial General Headquarters and of all Japanese armed forces and all armed forces under Japanese control wherever situated.

We hereby command all Japanese forces wherever situated and the Japanese people to cease hostilities forthwith, to preserve and save from damage all ships, aircraft, and military and civil property and to comply with all requirements which may be imposed by the Supreme Commander for the Allied Powers or by agencies of the Japanese Government of his direction.

We hereby command the Japanese Imperial General Headquarters to issue at once orders to the Commanders of all Japanese forces and all forces under Japanese control wherever situated to surrender unconditionally themselves and all forces under their control.

We hereby command all civil, military and naval officials to obey and enforce all proclamations, orders and directives deemed by the Supreme Commander for the Allied Powers to be proper to effectuate this surrender and issued by him or under his authority and we direct all such officials to remain at their posts and to continue to perform their non-combatant duties unless specifically relieved by him or under his authority.

We hereby undertake for the Emperor, the Japanese Government and their successors to carry out the provisions of the Potsdam Declaration in good faith, and to issue whatever orders and take whatever action may be required by the Supreme Commander for the Allied Powers or by any other designated representative of the Allied Powers for the purpose of giving effect to that Declaration.

We hereby command the Japanese Imperial Government and the Japanese Imperial General Headquarters at once to liberate all allied prisoners of war and civilian internees now under Japanese control and to provide for their protection, care, maintenance and immediate transportation to places as directed.

The authority of the Emperor and the Japanese Government to rule the state shall be subject to the Supreme Commander for the Allied Powers who will take such steps as he deems proper to effectuate these terms of surrender.

Signed of _____ TOKYO BAY, JAPAN _____ at _____ 0904 I _____

on the _____ SECOND _____ day of _____ SEPTEMBER _____, 1945

重光葵

By Command and in behalf of the Emperor of Japan
and the Japanese Government.

梅津美治郎

By Command and in behalf of the Japanese
Imperial General Headquarters.

Accepted at _____ TOKYO BAY, JAPAN _____ at _____ 0908 I _____

on the _____ SECOND _____ day of _____ SEPTEMBER _____, 1945

for the United States, Republic of China, United Kingdom and the Union of Soviet Socialist Republics, and in

the interests of the other United Nations at war with Japan.

Douglas MacArthur
Supreme Commander for the Allied Powers

C.W. Nimitz
United States Representative

徐永昌
Republic of China Representative

Bruce Fraser.
United Kingdom Representative

Kuzma Derevyanko
Union of Soviet Socialist Republics
Representative

E.A. Blamey
Commonwealth of Australia Representative

Moore Cosgrave
Dominion of Canada Representative

Leclerc
Provisional Government of the French
Republic Representative

C.E.L. Helfrich
Kingdom of the Netherlands Representative

Leonard M. Isitt
Dominion of New Zealand Representative

44

Only this text in English is authoritative

ACT OF MILITARY SURRENDER

1. We the undersigned, acting by authority of the German High Command, hereby surrender unconditionally to the Supreme Commander, Allied Expeditionary Force and simultaneously to the Soviet High Command all forces on land, sea, and in the air who are at this date under German control.

2. The German High Command will at once issue orders to all German military, naval and air authorities and to all forces under German control to cease active operations at **2301** hours Central European time on **8 May** and to remain in the positions occupied at that time. No ship, vessel, or aircraft is to be scuttled, or any damage done to their hull, machinery or equipment.

3. The German High Command will at once issue to the appropriate commanders, and ensure the carrying out of any further orders issued by the Supreme Commander, Allied Expeditionary Force and by the Soviet High Command.

4. This act of military surrender is without prejudice to, and will be superseded by any general instrument of surrender imposed by, or on behalf of the United Nations and applicable to GERMANY and the German armed forces as a whole.

- 1 -

5. In the event of the German High Command
or any of the forces under their control failing
to act in accordance with this Act of Surrender,
the Supreme Commander, Allied Expedtionary Force
and the Soviet High Command will take such punitive
or other action as they deem appropriate.

Signed at *Rheims at 0241 France* on the 7th day of May, 1945.

On behalf of the German High Command.

[signature: Jodl]

IN THE PRESENCE OF

On behalf of the Supreme Commander,
Allied Expeditionary Force,

[signature: W. B. Smith]

- 2 -

On behalf of the Soviet
High Command,

[signature: Souslaparof]

[signature]

Major General, French Army
(Witness)

US COAST GUARD

Brownsville, Pennsylvania is beside the Monongahela River, flowing north from West Virginia to Pittsburgh. Before 1960, to cross the River, it was necessary to go over the Inter County Bridge. The bridge is a well built structure that bore the full load of traffic along Route 40, the first National Highway that went from the East Coast to the West Coast of the United States.

When I was seventeen years old, living on the South Side of Brownsville, the object of my affections lived across the River on the West Brownsville side.

One warm summer afternoon, I decided to go across the bridge and visit the young lady, a surprise visit. What I learned made me realize you do not make a surprise visit to a member of the opposite sex.

While in the middle of the bridge, I noticed a nice boat on the West Brownsville side of the River. It was a cabin cruiser of some sort and flew a odd looking flag. The red stripes were vertical instead of horizontal!

To go down to the beach for a better look, it would be out of my way. But, I stopped walking, leaned on the railing and took a good look at the vessel that had just pushed its bow onto the sandy beach.

It was white and about 35 to 40 ft long. Before the engine stopped, the exhaust sounded very deep throated and powerful. My body felt the vibrations of the exhaust.

The boat did not resemble anything I had ever seen. It certainly was not a civilian boat but I didn't recognize it as a military craft.

Three crewmen, dressed in blue dungarees and shirts, came out of the boat's cabin. A fourth man came up from what was probably the engine room. He was dressed similar to the others, except for one minor difference. Three of the four had the little white hats that sailors wore. While one seemed to be

US Coast Guard 38' patrol boat.

Brownsville, PA from West Brownsville, PA.

checking out the lines, the second and third one was tying the boat to a rock. The fourth had a tan official looking hat with a gold badge on the front. They were obviously military. Again, I looked at the flag, it was very unusual.

As the three sailors were securing the bow to the big rock on the beach with a rope (It was actually called a "line".) their attention was diverted to the cement steps that came down from the bridge to the beach. There was loud feminine talking and laughing coming from two young girls walking toward the boat.

The girls were too far away for me to positively identify but they looked familiar. When the girls got to the boat, they went up a little ladder, helped aboard by the sailors. Then, they all disappeared down into the long cabin.

What was this boat? Who were the crew? What was that odd flag that it flew? Why were they here? At a distance, the girls reminded me of two of my friends, but it was too far to positively identify them.

I was too young to realize the ramifications of what I just witnessed, I shrugged it off and continued across the bridge to the West Brownville side and walked to the home of my heart throb.

After I knocked on the screen door, her mother came, appeared surprised and asked me why I had not called first. Being immature and not recognizing obvious signs, I asked if the young lady was home. Her mother answered, "She is with her cousin, LuAnne." "They are busy this afternoon. You should call before walking all the way from South Brownsville." She smiled, and then left the doorway.

To make the trip worth while, I went nearby to visit my buddy Ken Rinehart. Ken and I had a cup of coffee and sat on the porch talking about hunting and chasing girls. That reminded me of the mysterious boat. He informed me it was a 38 foot long US Coast Guard Picket boat that patrolled the river. The crew checked the river locks, buoys and anything that might be out of order on the waterway.

That style of boat was built during Prohibition to chase whiskey runners on the lakes and rivers. During the war they were used for different patrol duties. In the neighborhood where Ken lived, there were many men who worked on the tow boats on the Monongahela, they talked about such things.

As I was a curious young man who was interested in boats and girls, the connection between what I observed from the bridge came together. Neighborhood girls would pass the word around when the boat came to West Brownsville and they would go down to visit the young Coast Guardsmen.

Some way, I wanted to verify one of my suspicions. On the way back to the bridge, I turned left and walked down the street nearest the river. There were homes, bushes and trees among the houses and the beach. When I found a suitable spot where I could get a better look at the boat, I stopped.

It was not a long wait. Soon, I heard more girls going down the beach to the boat. They too went up a little ladder and down in the cabin. Then, the two original girls came out, down the ladder and back down the beach.

The girls were talking and laughing. They were the object of my desire and her well endowed cousin LuAnne!

I had to find out what was going on. After the girls were out of sight, I crossed the beach to the boat. While looking at it from stem to stern, scrutinizing every bolt and rivet and trying to give the appearance that I knew what I was doing, one of the white hat sailors, with bell bottomed blue jeans, came out and asked me if I would like to come aboard.

The sailors were young, kind and polite. They asked me how I liked the boat, why was I interested in small craft and would I like a cold Coke and tour the craft.

The boat had been refitted from a Picket boat to a proper craft for the job it was assigned. There was a head (Toilet) up in the bow; the bridge held all the equipment necessary to pilot the craft.

The guide explained to me the boat was a 38 foot Picket boat with a Murray and Tregurtha Model K, a 6 cylinder engine that produced 325 horsepower. They needed this type of boat and motor to chase whiskey runners and other criminals. That sounded interesting but I wanted to see the cabin.

There was a door in the back of the pilot house that lined up with a door going into the main cabin.

The cabin was sparsely equipped but it did the job. Bottle gas operated refrigerator, stove and lights. Some cabinets to store food and other items and four fold down single bunks, two high. A small steel table with a rim around the edge completed the cabin. Everything was spotlessly clean.

While looking around the living space, I saw the other two girls. They were sitting there, drinking coke and talking with the two other younger sailors. The fourth sailor was obviously the commander of the crew of three. He had the big tan hat and was older than the other three sailors.

After I mentioned the two girls that had left, the obvious commander said, "Yes, they are nice young ladies. Those two just had their 18th birthdays. I don't permit guests younger than 18 years old aboard."

He must have noted my surprised look. He then asked me if I knew the two. My answer was an affirmative. I then blurted out, "But, they are only fifteen years old!"

The commander gulped, his face got red. He said, "OH DAMN! They told me they were 18! I can get in BIG trouble letting them aboard! From now on, I will ask anybody who comes aboard how old they are and must be able to prove it!"

I smiled, knowing I had stopped something I was jealous of!

Then, the commander looked at me, directly in the face and asked me how old I was. When I stuttered out "Seventeen," He told me to get OFF his boat and not come back until I was old enough.

While walking home with mixed feelings about what I had experienced, what became plain to me was that if I wanted girls, I should become a Coast Guardsman! In addition to working on small craft, girls would make it very exciting.

The next day, after doing some inquiries, it became clear that the US Coast Guard was not interested in recruits my age. The legal age to enlist in the Coast Guard was twenty one. The age level could be dropped to 18 if the parents of the proposed recruit would sign the enlistment papers.

Naturally, I asked both of my parents if they would sign for me. At the same time, they exclaimed, "YOU CAN'T SWIM!" After that, both of them emphatically said "NO". I began to look for other angles.

In another year, when I wanted to enlist in the military, the memory of girls being attracted to sailors, bell bottomed trousers, good stories about boats and being able to travel to other countries appealed to me. All the above with three square meals a day, clean place to sleep and hot showers convinced me where to go.

It was a natural for me to enlist in the United States Navy!

BOOT CAMP SERVICE WEEK

As a child in the Great Depression, I was a finicky eater. There were many things that did not appeal to my taste. Our family's financial situation was like others of the times, we did not have enough money for expensive food. We dined on the very basics. Mother used to take a pot outside and pick Dandelion and Polk leaves for salads. This was taking things too far for my palate.

When these inexpensive salads were in front of me at meals, I would not touch them even though they were doused with salad oil and spices. Mother tried to have meat once a day. There would be four of us at the table. That meant there would be four small pieces of meat. If there were ever five pieces, Dad would get the extra piece because he worked hard in the mines. We all understood that.

Personally, I would rather go hungry than eat "weeds". This would ire my parents who were very thrifty. They would explain to me the benefits of eating greens, my growing body needed more than meat and potatoes. My Mother would also explain that in that era we were lucky to have what was placed in front of us. One of her arguments was, "There are starving children in China that would love to have anything at all to eat!"

My hard working Dad would become irritable and exclaim "SOMEDAY YOU WILL BE EATING OUT OF GARBAGE CANS!" It would not sway my opinion of the meal. I used to think, "Why did we reach the top of the food chain and still eat WEEDS?"

As the years went by, my boney frame grew taller but without the proper nutrition. One result was my legs became very bowed. But, I still would not eat those weeds.

Years later, I enlisted in the US Navy. While in Boot Camp at Great Lakes Training Base in Illinois, it was our Company #291's turn to do a week for Mess Hall Service duty.

We Boots were divided among the duties. Some went to the mess hall to serve food, some to the sculleries and some outside to the garbage disposal building.

I was sent to the food preparation area. There, we received many large, one hundred pound sacks of excellent Idaho potatoes. They were very big and prime. To remove the peels, they were dumped into large machines that had interior rough, rotating tubs. When the potatoes were in and the lid secured, the potatoes would spin around the tub. The rough tub would rub off the skins. The proper sequence was to dump the skinned potatoes into pans in front of us. We were equipped with table spoons that were sharpened around the edges. With these implements, we dug out the eyes of the potatoes and then dumped them into tubs for the kitchen.

However, one ingenious sailor thought of a better idea. He left the potatoes spinning in the tub until they were smaller, worn down to where the eyes were ground off. Then, unload them directly into the tub to be taken to the kitchen.

This seemed like a good idea. However, most of the potatoes would be ground off. The result would be, the potatoes would be very small. The majority that was ground off was then flushed down the drain. This was a great waste of expensive Idaho potatoes.

One day, a cook came in to find out why the big potatoes were just small potatoes when they got to the galley. The little potatoes were not enough to feed all the hungry sailors in the mess halls. He checked several times before he really found out what was going on. He went for the Chief Cook and brought him in. The Chief was so angry over the expensive trick that was being played; he dispersed us to different jobs around the mess hall.

I was sent to the garbage house. That was considered as the lowest job in the mess hall system. Outside of the mess hall and across the street was the smelly, undesirable garbage house.

Our job was to receive the many garbage cans that were filled with refuse from the mess hall, dump the cans into dumpsters and then steam clean the cans to be reused in the mess halls. Most of the time the cans were filled

with stinky, smelly stuff that was cleaned from the mess trays. Other times, it would be the grease from the pits under the ovens.

In boot camp, the mess halls really did not know how many people they would need to serve each day. The communication between the receiving part of the boot camp and the galley was sometimes very confusing due to the erratic influx of men as the Korean War began to escalate. The navy never served left over food. That meant that all the excess food had to be disposed of.

Sometimes it would be fresh baked buns, biscuits or warm bread. On a good day, different kinds of pies and cakes. Several times, nice big fully cooked roasts would be in the garbage cans. These were what I never got at home and here they were. All the GOOD things to eat! We all had pocket knives and used them to cut generous portions of the great food that came out for us to waste by throwing them into the garbage dumpsters!

One day, the Mess Bakers opened many gallon cans of cherries in anticipation of making Cherry pies. They had opened too many cans resulting in several garbage cans full of beautiful sweet cherries! I love cherries and began to eat them by dipping both of my cupped hands right into the garbage can and then directly into my mouth. They were delicious!

We soon realized we could eat quite well from the garbage cans and we did not need to stand in chow lines. Most of the time, the food in the garbage cans was excellent! We all took advantage of the great situation.

At that time, my Fathers' words came to me, "Someday you will be eating out of garbage cans!" One of the guys had a camera that day. After the photos were developed, he showed pictures of me not only eating out of garbage cans and drinking milk from a big can!

My Father was really surprised when I took those photos home and showed them to him.

Like most Fathers would, he had a great big smile as he said, "SEE, I told you so!"

DUTY AT NAVAL AIR STATION, MEMPHIS

Naval Air Station Memphis (NAS Memphis) was an exceptional place to serve while in the US Navy. The location was great due to weather, proximity to Memphis and wonderful Southern people. It was what we called "Good duty".

When I arrived in late November of 1950, the weather was warm and nice to be outside. It was much better than the cold and freezing Boot Camp in Northern Illinois. However, it soon got cold at Navy Memphis!

The job assigned to me was on the flight line. It involved directing aircraft moving around in the area around the hangars with a lighted, red wand in each hand and fueling aircraft from the gas truck, I soon learned that gasoline spilled on hands makes them REALLY cold. I became very careful.

Life in the barracks was not what you would expect. Living in those flimsy wooden structures that were hastily built in World War II for the influx of sailors to the air station, they were not insulated either in the walls nor the windows. We joked, "Those walls were so full of holes, you could throw a cat through them!" The only heat was potbellied stoves at each end of the building on each of the two floors. The cold winter wind would blow right through the walls. Ice covered the entire inside of the window panes. There were washing machines, if you wanted to call them that. They were so primitive they seldom worked and when they did, they jumped all over the floor. Electric or gas dryers were unheard of back then. We had to hang our wet clothes outside, summer and winter.

We slept on steel double decked bunks. In the winter, the lower bunks were very cold but the upper bunks were not quite as cold. In the summer, the opposite was true with the heat. Sometimes in the summer, it was so hot we could not get our white jumpers off. We had to sleep in them.

The men's rooms were communal. The shower room was large and had about 12 showerheads without dividers. The same lack of privacy existed in the room with the sinks and toilet stools. They were all side by side.

Our personal gear was perfectly placed in lockers. We passed inspections by placing all of our possessions on top of our bunks. We called those inspections, "Junk on the bunk."

As sailors, we found ways to make that way of life endurable. We played cards, shined our shoes and did our own ironing. We wrote a lot of letters to our parents, families, girl friends and to anyone who would answer.

Some of us were writing to several girls so a big problem was to make sure the proper letters got into the correct envelopes. That was always a potential problem for me since I was corresponding with several young ladies.

Of course, we went to Memphis at every opportunity. Some of us had cars and charged others to ride to town. After all, none of us made much money and car expenses were constant.

The kind people of Memphis made sure there were decent places of entertainment for sailors. There were two (United Service Organizations.) USOs and some of the churches had gathering places with bands and nice girls. I preferred the Salvation Army hall. They were nice enough to have private lockers for us to keep our civilian clothes. At that time, the military had to wear uniforms when entering or leaving the bases. Importantly, they seemed to have a better class of young ladies.

After I returned from Photo School, Bill Rowsey, a sailor from our Photo Lab became entranced with a beautiful girl. She was in a beauty contest. Bill took a 4X5 Speed Graphic to the affair and came back with a great photo of her in a white bathing suit. She was beautiful!

He wanted her to be at his side. He had a great idea that we helped him with. He had the very good large negative to work with. We took it into the photo print room, put it into a Omega D-2 Enlarger, turned the enlarger on its side by using the built in swivel. The image was projected onto the wall. Bill adjusted the height of the image to her exact size.

Bill had acquired a roll of photographic printing paper it was about two feet

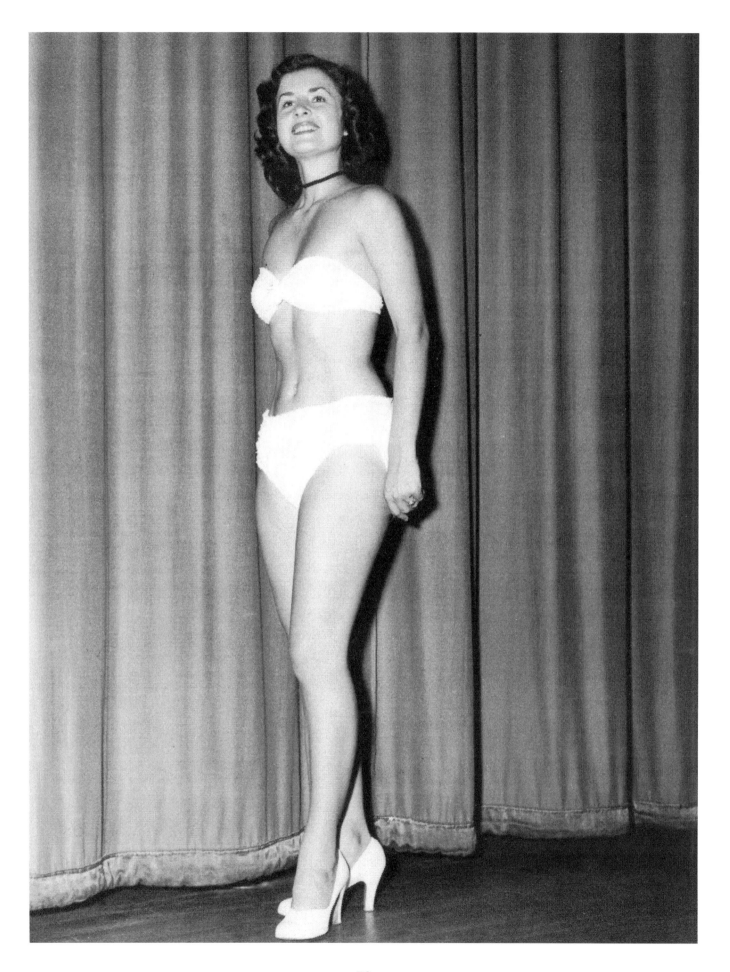

wide and six feet long. He taped the paper onto the wall, right where the image would be. We then exposed the full sized print, took it from the wall and laid it out on a darkroom table.

First Class Petty Officer Strickland had told us how to do this. Just about that time, he came in to make sure we did it correctly.

To develop the image, we had two trays of D-72 developer and some large cotton balls. We dipped the cotton into the developer and used them as swabs on the latent image. We had to put the developer on the paper evenly so it would all develop at the same rate. If one spot came up too quickly, Strickland had advised us of this possibility so we had prepared for it by having a tray of plain water. We would dip some of the water with another piece of cotton and dilute the developer on the "hot" spot. If a part of the print was a bit slow in developing, we would add more developer on the ball of cotton and rub the print.

The image came up and it was perfect! We then had to give it proper washing. We did that with a hose connected to a fresh water spigot with a spray attachment on the end.

We hosed the print down with fresh water for about a minute and then replaced the trays of developer with trays of Acid Fixer. We then used clean cotton to wipe down the beautiful photo. After completely stopping the chemical actions, we again hosed the print down for a half hour. This got the Acid Fixer off the print so it would not turn brown. Then, we hung it up to dry.

It turned out perfectly. Bill cut the image from the background and hung the curvy life sized image in the photo lab, on the back of a door in one of the film processing rooms. That was not a good idea.

The room would be dark when you entered it and continue to be kept dark while processing the film. But, when the safelight was turned on, out of the corner of your eye, the image of a person would appear and shock you.

We had to take the beautiful photo down from there. However, Bill had a solution. We had a bunk in the Lab for the Duty Photographer. Bill took the photo and taped it horizontally on the wall alongside of the mattress. Bill spent a lot of time in that bunk, looking at the beautiful girl who in his mind, was laying there beside him!

One day our Photo Officer pulled a surprise inspection on the Photo Lab, saw the lovely girl in the white bathing suit lying beside the bunk. He complimented us on our work but said it "…has to go…" Ruefully, we took it down.

Fortunately, Memphis was full of pretty girls!

The girls were lovely Southern Belles. We sailors and Marines were privileged to meet such genteel ladies. We enjoyed the town much better when we had a place to go to dance and meet with girls who we knew. We kept on our best behavior. The girls responded accordingly.

Several of the sailors married those nice young ladies from the Salvation Army. I was dating one of them. She invited me to her home only one time. As we were sitting in the kitchen, I saw something moving up the wall. It surprised me. I was unaware of the little things that ran around in the southern homes. But when she pointed out the window and said, "Do y'all see the pig pen right thar? Daddy said you and I could have that property to build our home on after we get married!" After that night was over, I never went back.

Life as a Navy Photographer was much easier than working on the Flight Line or Mess Cooking. We photographers spent most of our off hours in the lab. It was easier to type letters there than to hand write them in the barracks. The locks on the photo lab door made it secure enough to play cards for money. Hot coffee was always available.

After all, before I went to photo school, it was my job to keep the coffee mess well supplied and to keep the coffee pot going with good, hot coffee. I had friends in the mess hall.

Earlier, during my three month stint mess cooking, the cooks discovered I was from Southwest Pennsylvania. Most of them were from that area. My

The young ladies of the Salvation Army.

Mess Hall cooks.

origin was discovered when I called a paper bag a "poke". They took a liking to me and encouraged me to forget my desire to be a photographer and to become a cook. They encouraged me in any way they could. They would put me on preferable jobs and other favors. After leaving the mess halls, we continued our friendship. This resulted in my being able to "acquire" all the coffee making supplies I needed for the photo lab.

The photo lab crew at Memphis was the best I have ever worked with. The Leading Petty Officer was Aerial Photographer First Class (AF1) Victor S. Strickland, a great leader of men. He set a good tone to the working environment of the Photo Lab. He was a great mentor for the next few years as he preceded me to the USS YORKTOWN CVA-10.

The two and a half years spent at NAS Memphis were good years. Of course, part of that was the four months when I went to the Naval Aviation Technical Training Unit (NATTU) at the Pensacola Photo Schools. That was another great experience.

Memories of serving our Country are cherished by me; the time at Navy Memphis is very close to my heart.

My duties there, the experiences, girls, other photographers, the flying and partying in Memphis are some of the fondest memories of my long, exciting life.

US Navy School of Photography at Pensacola, FL.

PHOTO SCHOOL

After enlisting in the Navy, I was sent to Naval Air Station, Memphis, Tennessee. I worked on the flight line all winter. It was the coldest winter on record for the area. In the spring of 1951 I was sent to the galley for three months Mess Cooking. I had no idea what that meant.

After reporting to the Galley, I was assigned to the food preparation area, operating the potato peeling machine, then, to the Scullery. During this time, I was told that any man who worked three months at Mess Cooking was eligible for any "A" School in the Navy.

I wanted to fly and knew a bit about photography. That seemed to be a good rating I should try for. I applied for Photographic "A" School in Pensacola, Florida. After the stint in Mess Cooking, I was sent to work in the base Photo Lab until my orders to the Photo School came through.

While working in the photo lab, I found out thee were two kinds of Navy Photographers. The "PH" rating was for General Photographers. The "AF" rating was for aerial photographers. I knew which I wanted to be. From that time on, I signed all my paperwork as "AFAN". That meant I was a designated AF person. It worked! When my orders came through, it was for AFAN Richard G. Wells! I went to Naval Air Technical Training Unit (N.A.T.T.U.) at Pensacola for Photo School!

Photo students were housed in an old ante-bellum Southern home. It was a good time in our lives. The Enlisted Men's Club was close by; the classrooms were right near the beach. It was a great school and we learned a lot about photography. The basics were loading 4X5 inch cut film, exposure, shutter speed, depth of field, composition, still and motion picture shooting, processing, chemical mixing and printing.

It was such good training that the Motion Picture Industry and the National Space Agency hired former Navy photographers.

Photo "A" School was for basic photography. Those who were in the top 1/3 of the class or designated "AF" Strikers went to the Aerial "AF" phase. That included me. I was going to FLY!

Originally, when the class first opened, we had been split up in teams. One of the team members was AFAN Richard Straka. He and I were former Boy Scouts and had a lot in common. We became very good friends.

When in the motion picture phase, Straka and I led the team writing, scripting and shooting a movie about a shipwrecked girl. (We found a WAVE who would work with us.). We stayed together during the aerial phase and became friendly while flying and making aerial mapping runs.

When flying in the little SNJs with the open rear cockpit, we were held in by a "Gunners Belt." That was risky but fun. The Gunners Belt was a sturdy four inch wide leather strap fastened tightly around the photographer's waist. Attached to that strap were two one inch straps that had snap hooks that attached to special eye bolts inside of the aircraft. When flying maps, we flew in the twin engine, silver Beechcraft. That was a great utility airplane for the Navy.

We studied, swam and played on the pure white sand and in the beautiful warm water of the N.A.T.T.U. area. That is until a dead three foot long Barracuda washed up on the beach. After looking at those rows of sharp teeth, none of us went back into the water!

For the Christmas vacation of 1951, I could not afford to go home. I stayed on the base to study. However, a buddy of mine just bought a brand new, black Ford Convertible. On January 1, 1952 we put the top down and took a ride to Mobile, Alabama. We indulged in the two things that sailors on Liberty enjoyed the most!

On January 2, it was back to business.

We had classes about the large, bulky and heavy aerial cameras. Proper loading the big film magazines with the one foot wide and 100 feet long rolls of film was important. We also trained with the smaller thirty five pound F56 and the light 4X5 negative sized K20 cameras. The last two of these were hand held. The K20 was very simple and durable.

Then, we began the flying stage. WOW! My dreams were coming true. Flying obliques in the SNJ low wing, single engine planes was really fun. The after (rear) part of the canopy slid forward to enable us to take photos out the side of the airplane. We took high and low angle shots, using yellow filters, correcting the shutter speeds and sweeping the camera. One day, I took a low altitude oblique of my (then) girl friend out in her yard hanging clothes to dry in the hot sun!

Mapmaking was much different. It required a crew to do a correct flight in the reliable JRB or SNB twin engine, twin tailed silver Beechcrafts. The mapping planes had a hatch in the inside deck. A NR-1 mount was over the hole to hold the bulky aerial camera. There was an intervoltometer to control the shutter. It was set up for each picture to have a 65% overlap over the prior shot. This way, when making the map, we would only use the center portions of the print to eliminate linear distortion..

There were two problems. The photographer was in charge of the aircraft. When I gave the pilots directions, my stuttering made it difficult for me. However, the pilots were understanding gentlemen and helped me quite a bit. The second problem was that for a Aerial Photographer to complete the class, he had to be a Class B Swimmer. I could not swim.

That problem was solved when a buddy took my I.D. card to the pool and took the test for me. (That caused me a problem when I was a RECON squad leader in the Marine Corps.) I was able to graduate.

After the 16 weeks of photographic training, we were split up and sent to our next duty station. I was returned to N.A.S. Memphis Photo Lab at the Naval Air Reserve Training Unit (NARTU) and Richard Straka was sent there with me. This was done because the N.A.S. did not have as big a lab as the Reserve Center. All photographers, except the Identification Photo Lab on the South Side of the base, worked at the NARTU lab.

After passing the test for Aerial Photographer Third Class and "getting my

Author on a mapping flight in a twin engine JRB/SNB Beechcraft.

Crow" I flew in the little SNJ single engine aircraft to shoot many low level oblique photographs. Most of the time, after taking the assigned photos, the pilots would take short trips as a break in routine. That is when we did aerobatics such as inside loops, outside loops, Hammerhead stalls and inverted flight. That was FUN!

For mapping, we again used the twin engine Beechcrafts, the SNB or JRB. At the base we also had the PBY-5 Catalina Flying Boats. The big Plexiglas bubble on each side of those hulls made great camera stations. It was better than hanging by a gunner's belt. In addition, the PBY5 was a slow, lumbering camera station, much better for the slow shutter speeds of those days. I accumulated a lot of flight time in the amphibious PBY-5 but no landing or taking off on the water. I loved "stick time" in those big flying boats, day or night.

Of course, we flew other aircraft when it was convenient, most of the time the R4D (DC3), PB4Y-2 (B-24 with single vertical stabilizer).

Photo School and being an Aerial Photographer in the Navy made all my dreams come true! For the rest of my life, I have enjoyed photography and still LOVE to FLY!

THREE SCOUTS

In May of 1928, a newborn baby boy was left at the front door of St. Peters Orphanage in Memphis, Tennessee. He would never know his parents except for a few words on a form he received from the State.

The nuns at the orphanage were the only parents he cared to know. Sisters Barbara Spencer, Anna Jean, Joseph Agnes and others were his "parents".

As Frank Nobel grew up in the orphanage, he became part of it. He did everything he could to further the good of the institution. He became involved with the nearby Blessed Sacrament Catholic Church. He was generous in donating his time and meager savings to the Parish. For example, Frank paid for an $1800.00 alter rail and a $5700 used organ for the Parish.

When he was old enough, he enlisted in the Naval Reserve Training Unit in Millington, Tennessee. He became an Aviation Mechanic. During this time, he was active in the Boy Scouts. He became an Assistant Scoutmaster of Troop 63. He taught young orphan boys how to play baseball and football. Frank grew up to be a model citizen, sailor, mentor to young people and a good Catholic.

In 1952, Life Scout Richard Straka was assigned to the Naval Air Station (N.A.S.) Memphis photo lab, located in the Naval Reserve Training Unit hangar. In the course of his duties, he met Frank Nobel. Because they had Scouting and clean living in common, they became lifelong friends. Straka also became involved with the Boy Scout troop of St. Peters Orphanage and helping the kids while he became an Eagle Scout. Both of these fine young sailors spent many hours helping with the Catholic Church sponsored Boy Scout Troop.

Straka and I had been friends since Photo School at Pensacola, Florida. We understood each other because I had also been a Boy Scout and appreciated scouting life. We worked together on several photographic projects. I accepted him as a good sailor and great friend. Through Straka, I became a peripheral friend to Frank. He seemed to only tolerate me because I was a good friend of Straka. That was ok with me. Both were good company.

One day, Frank was visiting Straka at the Photo Lab. They discussed taking some of the orphan boys to a Boy Scout Camp for a day. I overheard the planning. It sounded like something that I would enjoy. I asked them if I could take part. They agreed. We were to take three of the boys to Camp Currier in Mississippi for a cook out, learn a bit about survival and to swim.

Early on a nice Saturday morning, we packed up two cars with three orphan scouts, Frank, Straka and I plus the camping gear for one day. Of course, we had ample food and our swimming gear. When we got to the camp we anxiously unloaded all the gear and set up camp.

While I picked up branches and built a fire in the pit, Straka began to set up the grill. Frank was busily teaching a bit of woodcraft to the young scouts. Everything was going great. After we had burgers with all the fixings, soda pop to wash it down, we cleaned things up and impatiently waited for a hour to pass before swimming.

Both Frank and Richard were good swimmers. I was not. The only way I could swim was underwater, as long as my breath held out. I knew the water was not over four feet deep so I felt secure and jumped in feet first. While splashing around, I noticed a log that had fallen into the stream. It was about 18 inches in diameter. One end was on the bank and the other end was in the water at the far side of the 15 ft wide stream. I could feel under the log, it had some water below it on the end near the bank, enough clearance for me to swim under it.

I submerged and began to swim underwater and under the log. I got about half way through the underwater space. My head was not yet above water when I felt a tug at the top of my navy blue swim trunks! Something had caught the trunks and I could not shake free. I began to panic! Because I was under water and the other guys busy with the chores, no body knew the difficult and potentially fatal spot I was in! Racing through my mind were things I might try to do. But no way could I get to the surface of the water! I

Giving back as always, Frank Nobel (left) was serving as scoutmaster of Boy Scout Troop 63 at St. Peter Orphanage in October 1953. Assisting was fellow Navy man Richard Straka.

Charles Nicholas
The Commercial
Appeal files

was being held by something! I had NO idea what it was! My air was running out. Something HAD to be DONE by ME! I then realized that even though my head was held under water, I could reach the surface.

Straka and Frank were at the campsite on the bank. I knew that and because I could reach the surface of the water. I put my hands up to be out of the water and began to splash. I was hoping they would hear the noise of the water or see the splashing. Straka had a Boy Scout Life Saving Badge and seeing the water splashing knew I was in trouble. He immediately jumped into the water beside me. He slowly and firmly told me "DO NOT GRAB ME!" Then he reached under the log, felt a stub of a 1 inch diameter branch that was stuck in my swimsuit. He released it and pulled me to the surface. I drew some good deep breaths of fresh air and was immediately grateful and forever thankful for the quick thinking of my friend Richard Straka.

Richard Straka, Frank Nobel and I still are in contact with each other and enjoy the friendship.

I personally honor those two Scouts!

They exemplify what Scouting is all about!

There are three basic reasons why boys join Scouting. The first is to gain access to things that interest them in the Merit Badge Program like woodcarving, types of collecting and involvement in things like photography.

The second reason is to join a gang. Boys enjoy the company of other boys and if it wasn't for Scouting, they could just as easily gravitate to less favorable gangs such as the Crips or Bloods.

The third reason they join Scouting is to have a way to vent their pyromania- this may SOUND bizarre, but have you ever noticed that men will sit around a campfire for hours, just staring into the flames and talking?

Scouting is many things to many people.

AGROUND!

"WELLS! YOU are the DUTY PHOTOGRAPHER TODAY! Get the standby camera and a film pack and report to the DUTY OFFICER. You are going on a little trip this afternoon!"

Strickland, the leading petty officer of the photo lab had received a request for a photographer to take some "grip and grins" off base. Because I had the task of being the Duty Photographer, it was my obligation to take any job that occurred out of the normal scope of our regular duties..

"WELLS! Before you go, get into your Dress Blues. You are going to Memphis for this special job!"

After reporting to the Naval Air Station Memphis Duty Officer, I was sent by official vehicle to the docks of Memphis to a Landing Ship Infantry! After reporting aboard, a Chief Boatswain Mate informed me that a contingent of city officials were coming aboard for a cruise on the Mississippi River and I was to record it for the local newspapers.

First of all, I had never been aboard a real Navy ship. This was all very new and exciting to me. The ship almost seemed alive! There were motors running, bells ringing, sailors and officers doing their jobs and everything seemed to mesh as one. The ship did not have a roll and pitch while we were tied up at the dock. The size of it was impressive, too. The biggest boat I had ever been on was Pip Caglia's canoe in the Monongahela River back when I was a kid. This Landing Ship really interested me. I couldn't wait to be able to look it over, from stem to stern!

After some untying of lines, blowing of whistles and motors running, we got under way. We pulled into the current and went upstream. We traveled about an hour up the Mississippi. Most of the guests were out on the Main deck.

The guests were the Mayor and City Commission of Memphis. To me, they seemed like a bunch of fat, grey old men, who were constantly smoking big smelly cigars.

With the low light of the day, the wet spray coming aboard over the bow and the general lack of cooperation of the guests, it was not practical to take photos with a 4X5 Speed Graphic. The Liaison Officer did not have the activity properly organized.

As a lowly Photographers mate, I did not have the authority to move those important people into position for a proper photograph.

When I asked the Liaison Officer what photos he wanted, he said, "When I need you, Ill let you know." I mostly stayed in his line of sight. He never called me.

Upstream of Memphis, the ship turned around and began to go downstream. I felt not needed and one of the sailors offered to take me on a tour of the ship. We went down a ladder (steel steps). When we got below decks and were looking at the sleeping compartments and the motors, we heard a lot of noise. It sounded like a big can opener was opening up the bottom of the ship. It was a very loud grinding and dragging noise. I ran to the ladder to get up to the main deck to find out what was going on. Then the whole ship lurched and stopped! Imagine, having never been on a ship before, making a good speed and then coming to a noisy, grinding, complete halt. As I scurried up the ladder, I held tightly to the rail with my free hand, to keep me from being thrown forward. Fortunately, the free hand kept me on the ladder. (In photo school, we were taught to always hold tight to the camera, so that it would never be dropped or lost.)

After recovering and getting up the next few steps, I was very worried. To a landlubber like me, it seemed the ship was ready to sink. Worst of all, I had not seen even ONE lifejacket! A Boatswain Mate was hurrying by. I grabbed him and excitedly asked, "WHAT is going ON?" He shrugged me loose and as he was hurrying away, snarled, "We hit a sandbar!"

The ship was on a steep angle. While hanging on the railings, working my way to the area of the bridge, I noticed the civilians were there. I got closer and heard them talking about what happened. One of them had asked if they could "...steer the boat..." Permission was granted. Then the rest of them, about ten, asked if they could also steer. Then, the Mayor of Memphis stepped forward and asked. He was given priority and went to the wheel. No doubt he felt he could handle it without any instruction and then began to wiggle the helm (steering wheel) without consulting the Navy Quartermaster who was trying to coordinate the steering situation without being obtrusive, was being questioned about some minor thing and could not pay enough attention to the Mayor. Then it happened.

The Mayor steered the boat, paying no attention to the buoys which marked the channel. He ran over the buoys. (That is what made the racket below decks. The buoys were anchored with chains to the bottom of the Mississippi River. With both the buoys and the chains rattling against the bottom of the hull, it seemed we ran over rocks.) The ship then hit shallow water and ran up onto a sand bar that was under the surface of the water.

A Landing Ship Infantry is built to run aground. It can absorb the shock of being grounded. It has twin propellers to aid in the backing down from such a predicament.

The Captain ordered the Helmsman back to the wheel and gave the order to back down both screws. The order was given and the ship shuddered but would not back down. The order was then given to give the engines full power to back off the sandbar. We could hear the powerful engines from the bridge (Wheelhouse.) Still nothing. We were stuck fast. The pressure of the flowing Mississippi River kept pushing the ship farther on the sandbar.

The Captain gave the order to reverse one propeller and the other propeller to be pushing foreword. That would make the ship wiggle a bit. Then, the engines were reversed in their pulling and pushing. Then, both engines were put in reverse. We didn't move off the bar. The Captain was notified the river level was dropping, making our predicament even more noticeable. The ship was really beginning to list (Tilt.). About that time, I was looking for a life preserver. After all, I could not swim!

In a combat situation, when a Landing Ship Infantry got two or one hundred yards close to the beach, the stern anchor would be released, drop to the bottom and hold fast. Then, when the ship wanted to back down from the beach, the anchor line would be winched in to pull the ship to deep water by holding to the anchor imbedded in the bottom. But this situation was due to an accident and the stern anchor had not been dropped.

A radio distress call was put to the US Coast Guard to send a tug boat out and pull the ship off. However, it was busy and would not be able to come out until after midnight. The river level was lowering. It became dangerous to even try to walk about. Some way, we had to rescue the civilians. The fat old men were chomping their cigars and looking confused.

Someone on the beach had a bright idea. There was a Coast Guard Auxiliary group in Memphis. They were telephoned and asked if they could help. They only had a small, private craft, too small to pull the ship out into deeper water but they could send it to try to take the non Navy personnel off the ship and to safety.

As we waited for the Coast Guard Auxiliary to spring to action, to get to their boats, find out where we were suppose to be and then rescue us, the River kept receding. In over an hour, the Coast Guard Auxiliary boat reached us. The small boat tied up to our lee side, as it was very close to the water, rigged up a ladder and took aboard the group of the old, grouchy, cigar chomping civilians.

I was not asked aboard the small boat because it was overloaded and I was not a civilian. By the time the tow boat came, pulled us off the sand bar and we returned to the dock, it was about 0400 (Four a.m.)

I was exhausted, staggered down the gangway and back to the Navy car that was to return me to the base. The BMSN (Boatswain Mate Striker.) driver began to chew me out for being so late. I was in no mood to listen to that. I told him, "Shove off Coxs'n, your boats' loaded!"

He did not expect "salty" talk like that from a photographer. He drove back to the base in silence. Dawn was breaking when we got back to the Naval Air Station in Millington.

When I returned to the Photo Lab, nobody was in the Duty Photographers bunk. I dropped into it and slept until the Photo Crew showed up. Petty Officer Strickland took one look at me and asked, "WHAT in HELL happened to YOU?" After I told the story, he laughed and told me to develop the film I had taken. He had to see the prints before actually believing me!

After all, how many sailors are actually aboard a ship that accidentally runs aground!

(Tied to buoys in Sasebo Harbor, the Yorktown became loose from one of them and swung around to a point where we only had a fathom 'six feet' of water beneath our keel. But, that's another story.)

SAILORS OF THE 1950S

The sailors, with whom I associated, generally seemed to have three major things in mind.

First, Women, after all, we would be apart from them for days, weeks and months at a time. Our average age was about 21 years old. All things being normal, this can be expected.

Secondly, Alcoholic beverages. These would be a poor substitute for the aforementioned women, but even when the women were available, alcohol had its use. (Candy is dandy but Liquor is quicker.)

Duty. WE ALL had to do our duty as Sailors and defenders of our Flag and Country. If we did it well, we would be able to get the first two of the three. If we did not do our duty well, we would get less.

This is simple. But, when you mix young women, alcohol and young men, many things happen. Some good, some not so good.

The first instance is about a very good young sailor. He did not drink, smoke or swear. He was an Eagle Scout and you could take his word as his bond. He worked hard and walked the right path.

However, one evening when some of us from the Photo Lab were getting ready to "hit the beach." (In sailor slang, that meant going into town, to chase girls and/or drink.) As we were getting into two cars to head South down the Dixie Highway to Memphis, the Eagle Scout asked if he could go with us. We consented.

The first place we stopped was our favorite joint near the Hotel Claridge. It was a quiet little bar where our group was well known and tolerated (We were generous with tips.).

As we sat and drank our Miller, Budweiser and Schlitz, the Scout began to act in an odd way. He began to keep up with us, beer for beer. His face was getting flushed. Our Leading Petty Officer liked cigars and always had some. He offered cigars to all. The Scout took one. Prior to this night, he NEVER smoked, drank nor cursed. As he drank, smoked and began to loudly exclaim the word "SHIT!" we began to notice more of a big change in him. He began to flirt with the waitress. Compared to him, she was no "spring chicken".

All of his actions were very different than what he had ever displayed. I knew him the longest because he was in the same class as I at Pensacola Photo School. He had NEVER acted like this before! The waitress was very understanding. She had seen many other very young sailors get in this condition. She took a good, long look at him and made us all promise that we would take care of him and get him back to base safely. Of course, we promised that but did not promise to stop enjoying watching him, nudging each other and laughing.

I have known that Eagle Scout for 58 years and sincerely believe he has never been in that condition again!

The next story is a bit different.

Four of us Photo Mates were in another bar in Memphis. We were all in one booth. We knew the waitresses and they bantered with us every time we came in. Talking, teasing and a bit of physical contact once in awhile, probably because we all were young and appreciated life. They were very cute.

One particular night, we had been drinking more beer than usual, teasing the girls a bit more than before. In fact, it was more like a party (But we were paying for the beer.).

One of them was dancing ON one of the tables, pulling up her white dress seductively and with a BIG smile!

I was lifting a cute one up with my arms while singing off color songs to her. She was all smiles.

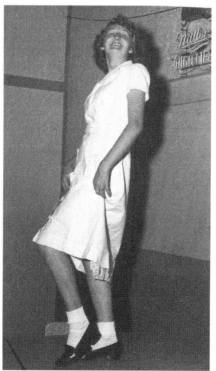

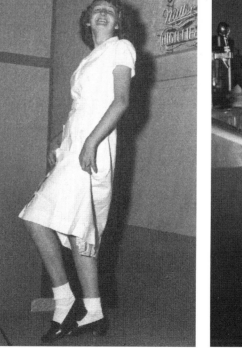

Dancing on the table.

After a few hours, one waitress must have become very tired, probably from getting up and down, dancing on the tables. She had lost some of her sense of humor. We sailors were in a booth. I was on the inside position, another was across the table from me and two were in the front part of the booth, where the waitress was standing.

One of the two sailors nearest her said something she disliked and she snarled, "BITE MY BUTT!" The sailor reached up with his arm, put it around her shoulders and pulled her, face down on the booth table top. While she was in the right angle, butt up and not being able to overcome the sailor's strength, he leaned over and bit her, HARD on her nearest cheek of her buttocks. After all, SHE asked for it!

As she screamed, he let her loose. She immediately stood straight up and began to scream, "SHORE PATROL! SHORE PATROL! Then even louder, "SHORE PATROL!" The two Shore Patrolmen, who were right out side the doors, watching us cavort, immediately ran into the bar.

As fast as we could, we four sailors staggered or crawled out of the booth, the other waitress shoved us toward the rear door, as quickly as she could. When we got outside, we four drunken sailors dispersed into the night. The Shore Patrol was running outside blowing their whistles and yelling "STOP! STOP!"

We made our escape. Next payday, we went back and along with the two waitresses, had a good laugh over the event.

But the waitresses never got that close to our booth again!

THE FIRST TIME ANY RUNWAY WAS FOAMED

Navy Aerial Photographer Jerry Crawford is the kind of guy that other guys like to have around. He is done many things as varied as rodeo riding, playing guitar, singing, building water boards to his first love, flying multi engine aircraft.

Jerry was from Texas and a very nice guy, full of jokes and with a big smile and cowboy hat to match. I have never seen him angry or distressed.

At Naval Air Station Memphis, where we both were stationed, his desire to be around aircraft drove him to change his rate to Air Controlman, Second Class. He was much happier in the Control Tower than in a Photographic Darkroom.

(After his hitch in the navy, he flew for several different people, including Burt Renolds. Later, he flew for and retired from Continental Airlines where he took a year leave to fly for Air America in Viet Nam. He was happy to get back to Continental Airlines because his airplanes did not suffer from bullet holes.)

When he had extra time, he would return to the photo lab to play cards with us and to tell of his times in the Control Tower.

For example, one day, he had a most exciting experience. A B-25 medium bomber pilot radioed to the Control Tower that the pilot could not get the nose wheel to lock in the down position. This would result in landing with only the two wheels that were located in the wings of the aircraft. This would cause the nose of the airplane to drop and be pushed along the rough surface of the runway. This situation would result in excessive damage to the Plexiglas nose of the aircraft and could possibly cause a very dangerous fire.

There was no precedence for this type of situation that would indicate how to enable to aircraft to land safely.

Jerry's quick mind had an unusual idea. The use of fire foam, up till then, was

8 October 2005

Federal Aviation Administration
800 Independence Ave., SW
Washington, D.C. 20591

Re: Runway Foaming for Disabled Aircraft

Dear Sirs:

I claim to be the first person to ever foam a runway for a disabled aircraft....This is the way it came about.

One summer morning in 1952 or 1953 at Millington , Tennessee I was the tower supervisor at NQA, the Navy Control Tower. I walked out on the catwalk that circled the tower and looked down below where the crash crew had spilled a patch of foam on the ramp. About the same time a massive 6 wheeled tug came around the corner and hit the foam. I was shocked to see the heavy vehicle spin out.

Curiosity got the best of me and I went down to talk to the crash chief. He explained that the foam was very slick and thick enough to smother a fire. I felt the foam and went on back to the tower cab.

Around noon we had a B-25 call in for landing and turning final the pilot reported that the nose wheel did not come down. He pulled up and went through his emergency procedures trying to get the gear down. After a short period of time the pilots decided the nose gear was not going to extend and we started considering options.

I got to thinking about the foam and knowing that the main gear on a B-25 is 20-25 feet apart, I wondered if he might be able to straddle a strip of foam down the centerline of the runway and drop the plexi-glass nose in the foam.. I reasoned that he would still have braking on the main gear and be able to keep a straight landing roll and the foam would cut down on sparks and the possibility of fire.

I talked to the duty officer downstairs and he told me to consult the pilot. They came back with, "We'll try anything, tower." I asked how long he could hold the nose off on landing and we had the crash crew spread an 8-10 foot wide strip of foam down the runway centerline starting approximately 2000 feet down the runway to about 4500 feet.

The pilots brought the B-25 in and dropped the nose in the foam stopping safely prior to the end of the foam. On inspection, it was noted that the plexi-glass was hardly scratched.

The two pilots bought me a case of scotch, and the Navy Department gave me a commendation for it. They sent a team down from Washington to collect data on the landing and came out with a Navy Tech order to consider foam in cases where an aircraft had gear problems.

I'm not the least bit interested in the scotch or the commendation, but at my old age I would like to have some documentation to leave for my children and grandchildren that I was the author of this procedure. My letters to the Navy Department have lead to them researching this story and all they could find was an article in the Navy Memphis paper....the Bluejacket about the event. They finally ventured this statement....."if you were the tower supervisor at Navy Memphis that day, you might indeed be the first person to come up with the idea of foaming a runway for a disabled aircraft.

Does the FAA keep any records on something like this? If there is any way for you to be of help in this matter it would be greatly appreciated.

Thank you for your consideration.

Yours very truly

J. H. Crawford, ATP1153152

to only pour it onto downed airplanes to prevent fires. Jerry knew the foam was slippery. He correctly reasoned it would put a soft, slippery covering for the bomber's Plexiglas nose to slide on.

He ordered the Naval Air Station Tower crash crew to spread foam on the middle of the runway to enable the airplane to put the nose down in the foam and possibly land safely. The bomber, while landing, kept the nose up as long as possible. When the twin motored bomber finally let down on the runway, the foam permitted the nose to slide until the aircraft came to a stop. This resulted in very little damage to the Plexiglas which was only lightly scratched.

This action by Jerry Crawford kept the plane from being greatly damaged and probably saved the crew from any injuries. He claims this was the first time foam was ever used in this manner.

Attached is the letter he had sent to the Federal Aviation Administration to verify his actions. FAA's answer stated that "someone" in the military was the first one to do this.

Jerry is now retired, living in his beloved Texas and has sport parachuted over 1,000 times!

SURPRISE!

At NAS Memphis, I had a short term friendship with a sailor named Stan. It was simple, I had a car, and he did not. He said he knew many women in Memphis, I did not. We formed an unholy alliance. The problem was, I didn't check him out before we began our adventures. I should have been leery. He was just an E3 Seaman with over eight year's service. That should have rang some bells.

He promised he would introduce me to women and get to a lot of parties. It sounded pretty good. We began our sorties into Memphis with high hopes.

We would scout the Peabody, Claridge and other hotel bars for target rich environments. But the ladies in elite bars would ignore sailors. Even in civilian clothes, our short haircuts made us obvious. The girls in the "sailor bars" would try to get us to spend our money with no reward. As a last resort, Stan would get out his "little black book."

He would telephone girls. (With my dimes!) It would take a while to get someone to go out with us. That should have rang another bell.

One night we hit the jackpot. One of the numbers he called told him that the lady in question was at a party. The phone number for the party location was given. Stan recognized the number and knew the house. We didn't call. (He had used up all my dimes.) We drove over there.

The house was all lit up, music coming out of an open window. We could see shadows moving around inside. When we opened the unlocked door and went in, it was like hitting the jackpot at Las Vegas. Women, wine, women, beer, women, music and more women! At first, I thought it might be a house of ill repute, but I was mistaken. There were very few guys and none in uniform. It seemed to be a place the locals kept quiet about.

Stan was a big guy and made a good first impression. He knew some of the girls who were not impressed. He introduced me to the ones he knew and it was up to me to take it from there.

After a few drinks, my speech problem seemed to clear up. The result was, my inhibitions began to disappear. They turned into ambitions. The more I drank the more fun I had.

Then, I began to notice couples were drifting off to different parts of the house. Then more did the same. After a while, they would come back out. I began to wonder what was going on and could not come up with a satisfactory answer.

Between the noise, dancing and coming and going, I soon lost track of who was with whom. It seemed to be all mixed up. It was very confusing.

It was pretty hard to figure out who I might be able to talk with and who was steady with someone that I should not talk to.

It was like being in the aforesaid Target Rich Environment but with no idea of who was who.

I figured I'd check out the girls who went with a partner and came back. I would stay away from any of them. I tried to figure out who did NOT go into the other part of the house with someone. But, the amount of alcohol I had imbibed was keeping me confused.

After a while, I don't know how long, Stan came around. I asked him what is going on. He laughed and said I had too much sex on my mind. It was all innocent. There was a pool table in one of the rooms and some slot machines in another. This was a party in someone's house who liked to make a few bucks at the party goers' expense. The pool tables had to be fed money, as the slot machines. The homeowner got the profits which paid for the beer. Liquor was being sold in one of the other rooms. That answered my questions.

Now, with my mind at ease I began to check out all the girls. They were happily drunk and dancing. The more I drank the better looking they got. Finally, I got the nerve to talk with one of them. She was a dark haired young lady with a great dimpled smile. She liked to talk, so I listened. I didn't have to talk which permitted me to hide my stuttering problem. She sat down beside

me and told me all about herself. She talked, I listened and we slowed down on our drinking and began to enjoy each other.

One of the girls brought a baby. The dark haired girl and I offered to hold it while the Mother was dancing. We had the little one for about an hour. It was the first baby I had held since enlisting in the Navy.

We got along so well that she gave me her name and the address of the YWCA where she was living. The following week, I was to pick her up for a date.

However, when I drove up to the front of the YWCA, I became so petrified that I would stutter when I went in to the greeting desk to ask for her. My fear of embarrassment was so great, it was impossible for me to get out of the car.

I sat there, in my car, disgusted with myself for a half an hour. Then, slowly I put the Chevy in gear and drove away. In a few days I struggled with a phone call to her. She expressed sympathy and understanding, but she broke off the budding relationship. I always regretted my failure to overcome my fear and go in the YWCA. She may have been waiting for me right inside of the front door!

In the wee hours of the morning, the party broke up. Stan and I had made some time with two of the ladies. I was in good with the dark haired girl and Stan had a tall blonde who owned the house. She invited Stan to stay the night. Stan asked, "How about my buddy?"

The blonde said she could fix up a place for me to sleep. I then looked around for the dark haired girl, but she had left with her girl friend that brought her.

I slept on a couch.

Before dawn, Stan and I got in my little Chevy coupe and began the drive back to the base. We were hung over and tired. When we were about there, Stan said, "Lookee here!" When I glanced over, he had a pair of black lace panties in his hands. I was surprised, asking "Where did you get THOSE?" He just smiled.

After we got on the base and while driving to our barracks, Stan said, "I've got an idea!" It was almost daylight and I didn't want to hear any more of Stan's ideas.

The Admiral of the Naval Air Training Unit at NAS Memphis had an Administration Building across the street from our barracks. Stan had the idea of running the sexy panties up the flagpole. I didn't immediately realize the penalty for such a stunt; I just wanted to get to my bunk. Stan talked me into saying "ok." We pulled up beside the flagpole. Stan got out, hooked up the flimsy black thing to the lanyard and hoisted them up to the top of the pole, ran back to the car and we sped across the street to our barracks.

We couldn't wait till eight o'clock when the Marines would be out to raise the colors for the day. We sat there and stifled giggles and laughter until the appointed time.

One minute till eight o'clock four Marines smartly came out of the Ad Bldg, two Marines with rifles and one Marine with the flag. The other Marine marched with them. They approached the flagpole and reached out for the snap hook to attach the flag. It was not there. The Marine looked up the lanyard and there, at the top of the Admirals' flagpole, fluttering in the breeze, was the pair of black lace panties!

From our hiding place behind a bunk, we could plainly see the disgust and anger the Marines had. There was not doubt that if they knew who did the dastardly deed they would immediately arrest the offender(s) and drag them to the brig, taking the LONG way to get to the place of confinement. .

No doubt if that would have happened, I would have lost my rating as Petty Officer and maybe some brig time.

At that time, I realized why Stan was still an E3 Seaman after eight years in the Navy. If I hung around with him, I would be a loser like him. That was not in my "game plan". That was the last of our association. I've always felt I was lucky to get away with that trick and decided Id never do anything like that again.

The really sad part of the story is never seeing the little dark haired girl again.

FLYING AT NAS MEMPHIS

The SNJ was a fun plane to fly, especially in the rear cockpit. Back there, I did not have the responsibility of the aircraft and how to get from point A to point B. That was for the pilot to think of. I was only ballast to enable the official pilot to fly the front seat.

This was fine with me. I could concentrate on what was happening around me. One bright afternoon, the pilot asked if I wanted to go someplace special. I told him no, but I would like some aerobatics. He seems surprised because most rear seat flyers do not like that sort of thing. It not only made them sick to the stomach and there was a greater element of risk involved. There are many things that could go wrong. I was willing to risk anything to fly.

Generally, I preferred to fly with Enlisted Pilots. At that time, the rate "Enlisted Pilots", was in effect. There were two of them; one had an Italian name that I have forgotten. The other one was Aviation Pilot Chief Poag. Chief Poag was what people think a Navy Chief should resemble. He was tall, light hair, slender with a everlasting smile. Even though he was a quiet person, he enjoyed a good joke. He was an excellent pilot in every way. I later found out he had been a combat fighter pilot in World War II.

When flying, APC Poag was cooperative. He did a few turns and then asked me if I liked to loop. Naturally, I did and told him that I enjoy inside and outside loops. He accommodated me and we did two of each. I think he expected me to call the game off. Then, I asked him about inverted flight. That was always a thrill.

When the plane is flying normally, your weight is on the seat. The shoulder straps are only there if needed. But, when inverted, your body weight is on the shoulder straps and your bottom is actually an inch or two off the seat. It is a strange feeling. To look at the ground, you look up and to see the sky would be looking down toward the bottom of the airplane. That was a favorite of mine.

Poag must have been thinking, "How can I scare this photographer?" He asked me if I had ever experienced a Immulman turn. Again, I had and told him so. All that was to me was turning the airplane 180 degrees. As a seemingly last resort, he asked "Have you ever done a Hammerhead Stall?" Well, he finally got the answer he wanted. I said "No.".

I can still remember the thoughts, "I'll bet Chief Poag is grinning!" He is going to give me a REAL ride!

He flew perfectly level and then increased his throttle to full and pulled the stick back to get the nimble little SNJ perfectly vertical. As we went straight up, he "chopped the throttle" to about ¼ and let the plane slow. It vibrated as we approached a full stall, I got very worried. The plane stopped it vertical ascent! We hung there for what seemed a second or two, then it began to drop backwards from the Heavens! Down and down, out of control! Pilot Poag then applied full right rudder with a little throttle. The plane rotated and went downward. After it seemed to drop a mile (Of course it didn't fall that far, but it felt like it.) he straightened the rudder, gave the engine some throttle and pulled up and leveled the plane. It was a very dramatic maneuver. (That was never in my Cub handbook.)

The pilot, with a bit of sarcasm in his voice over the intercom asked "How was THAT?" I answered, "Let's go back up for my stomach." . He laughed over that. Then, we flew straight and level for awhile. Which made me very thankful so I could get the butterflies in my stomach back in formation..

While we were flying low, straight and level, I looked down to the ground. I saw something that aroused my curiosity. There appeared to be very large white maggots with black heads crawling through the cotton field below and eating up the cotton balls! What could those be? I mentioned it to the pilot but he was too busy to check it out. Of course, he might have thought I was still disoriented from the last maneuver.

That night at a dance at the Salvation Army, I asked my Memphis girl friend about it and she got a big laugh out of that, but did not explain it to me.

PBY-5 amphibious flying boat.

SNJ and author.

Later, after she told all her girlfriends what I told her and they all giggled, she then told me what I actually saw.

When the cotton is ready to pick, the black workers are given large cotton bags. They range from five foot long for kids to use and seven feet long for the adults. They are about two feet across and have a shoulder strap to enable the picker to pull the bags while picking cotton with both hands. The more they pick, the more full, round and long they get. From the sky, they would resemble maggots with the black head of the "maggot" actually the head of the picker. As they would go through the field from a few across to many pickers lined up shoulder to shoulder, the field would appear full of cotton in front of the pickers. In back of them, not any cotton balls. It would appear the maggots were eating the balls. The girls would giggle and point at me the rest of the night. I know I heard the term "Damnyankee" used several times while referring to me.

The next day, the Chief Poag asked me if I would like to fly to Little Rock, Arkansas. Naturally, I said, "Sure, Chief!" He began talking to the control tower confirming the flight plans and we headed west. We were flying about 4,000 ft altitude. The sun was setting. After it went down below the horizon, the pilot asked, "Would you like to see that sunset again?"

I was a bit confused. How could I see it again? The pilot climbed altitude to about 2,000 more feet. The sun came back up and then as we dropped down again, the orange sun went down below the horizon again! To me, that was fantastic!

The pilot explained to me that he needed some night flying experience for his log book as we flew toward Little Rock. It was dark by the time we flew over the Arkansas city. As usual, I was very interested in the change of the colors and shadows at that time of day. The city darkened. I saw a collection of electric lights that puzzled me. It was a group of lights that just seemed to be zig zagging all over the place. Buildings and such have many lights but in an orderly fashion. These seemed to have no plan or reason. Just all over. Usually the pilots do not like to be distracted from flying but I asked about them. He looked out, laughed and said, "Those are lights are randomly stretched over used car lots." Ok, I understood that. But, it was something I would not have guessed.

The flight home in the night air was very boring. Blackness all around except for the navigational lights on the wingtips and the tail and the instruments. The noise of the engine was very loud. With nothing to look at and too much racket to sleep, time dragged on and on.

It was for the Chief, too. He asked me if I wanted to fly it for awhile? I jumped at the chance. I have had "stick time" before, by day but not at night. But this time, I was to hold the course and fly by instruments. The conditions were for me to keep the artificial horizon indicator flat and a bit above the horizon. The altimeter was to be kept at the same altitude. And, of course, to constantly watch the rest of the controls like oil pressure, compass and other gauges. It was easy compared to flying the beautiful PBY-5 Catalina Flying Boats.

(The Catalina's were a very slow moving aircraft, designed for over ten hours of non stop flying. They had a very slow airspeed and with the Flight

Engineer's tower above the cabin, that the high wing was attached, it was difficult to keep the plane level. It was at night and the artificial horizon kept moving all over the gauge. I kept compensating and compensating. But, it kept wallowing through the air like a slow moving 12 foot motorboat through water.)

(The pilot had gone aft for a sandwich and a coffee. He came back and asked me, "What he hell are you doing?" When he saw me compensating, he smiled and said, "In this kind of a aircraft, the artificial horizon WILL be all over the place. You must not over correct as you are doing. Just make sure you keep it above the moving horizon and maintain your altitude. It will be just fine. I am going back aft and play cards awhile. "After he gave that tip to me, the airplane flew very well with the minimum of stress on this enlisted aircrewman.)

I flew the little SNJ all the way back to Memphis Naval Air Station. The pilot took over the controls and landed. I became friends with the SNJ pilot. We flew together several times. I flew with Chief Poag until he got back his wartime commission to become Lt. Poag. About a year later, he died in a Grumman F8F, right near the runway at NAS Memphis.

The F8F was a short fighter plane with a big ten foot four bladed propeller. To enable the prop to clear the ground on such a short length airplane, it had to have long landing gear to have the correct angle. This made the plane difficult to see well enough to taxi properly.

Because of the lack of visibility from the cockpit, the pilot would need to weave as he taxied on the runway approach.

One day while weaving and taxing a F8F, Lt. Poag got too close to the edge of the cement. The wind was gusty and it pushed him sideways. One wheel went over the edge of the tarmac and was stopped when it hit the soft earth. The unstable aircraft tipped over. Lt. Poag was hanging by his harness, upside down over the ground, in the cockpit.

The crash crew was immediately sent out. The designers of the stubby plane

Lt. Poag's aircraft.

anticipated it tipping so they built a long tube running crosswise in the body of the plane, aft of the cockpit. This was to place a long metal bar through this tube, attach a chain to each end of the bar and lift the rear part of the plane. The short plane would automatically right itself. However, the crash crew didn't have the required rod. So they passed a chain through the tube.

It was a fatal mistake.

With the chain through the tube, when it was pulled upwards, it acted as a can opener on the fuselage's thin aluminum skin. The plane dropped back, upside down to the ground. But, it was wet ground because the crash crew was dousing the plane with fire foam and water to prevent it catching fire. Soft ground and water make mud. The big heavy engine began to sink into the mud. It took the rest of the aircraft with it. Deeper and deeper. Lt. Poag was still strapped in the pilot's seat, upside down. As the plane sank, unable to be pulled out, Lt. Poag's head touched the mud. He yelled to the crash crew of his predicament but he kept sinking lower and lower. By the time proper equipment arrived, Lt. Poag's head was submerged in the mud. He gagged and slowly suffocated.

I will never forget Lt. Poag.

THE ONLY PLACE FOR A SAILOR IS AT SEA

In spite of my repeated requests to be transferred to the Sixth Fleet in the Atlantic Ocean, the powers that ruled the US Navy decided they needed AF3 Richard G. Wells elsewhere.

In February of 1953 my orders arrived for me to report to the aircraft carrier, USS YORKTOWN CVA-10 of the Seventh Fleet in the Pacific Ocean!

The Sea actually fascinated me from my youth. The books of Jack London and others like him were treasured. Descriptions of the salt spray, changing colors of the salt water, flying fish and strange ports of call are things I dreamed of. Of course, the mysterious ladies in all those ports were beckoning to me.

My thoughts of visiting the European ports by the Atlantic were forgotten as the visions of Hawaii and the Pacific Rim changed my mind. After all, across the waters, golden beauties would be waiting.

Oh, I couldn't wait to see my first aircraft carrier and sail the magnificent Pacific Ocean!

After a short leave that enabled me to go home for a couple of weeks, I proudly boarded the airplane and went to California to report aboard the newly recomissioned fighting ship!

It was at night when I saw my new home for the first time. It was SO tall and SO long. It was over a THOUSAND FEET in length! The ship was lit up, new noises to my ears such as bells, squawk boxes, whistles, many electric motors humming. It was FANTASTIC! It seemed to be a living, breathing steel monster.

I reported aboard and was awed by the magnificence of a REAL fighting ship! Never had I stepped aboard a ship with a six inch armor plate deck, the top of its mast was taller than any building I had ever been in.

The whole ship was bright, clean and a wonderful sight. There was no doubt in my mind this would be one of my life's' greatest Experiences! For the next fourteen months that I was a crewmember, IT WAS!

I am still proud to be able to exclaim, "I am a YORKTOWN SAILOR!"

Replenishment of oil, food, and mail at sea.

A STUTTERING SAILOR

In the early 1950s, there were no provisions for people who stuttered. Persons who were so afflicted lived on the edges of society. They were not given the better jobs nor recognized as productive persons. When they did get a decent job, they did it quietly and usually unseen. Most were loners. However, there was an exception to the rule. I always wanted to see and do things! I wanted adventure!

My speech defect was stuttering and blocking. Many people know stuttering people but a few people also have blocks. This is a terribly demeaning thing. The throat and chest seem to seize, the jaws tighten and the eyes bulge. It almost seems like a fit. Someone who was not aware of blocking would be alarmed at the sight.

The Draft Board was getting close to me. That nudge gave me the excuse to enlist in the Navy. After barely passing the speech part of my physical, I was sent to the Naval Air Station at Memphis, Tennessee where I became an Aerial Photographer and a Combat Air Crewman.

For a person to have these problems and be in the military is a peculiar situation. After all, speaking can mean someone is in mortal danger. Adding to this, people who have this problem are usually considered inadequate in other areas. In all of my seven years in the military, I never met another person who stuttered.

A situation where speech was important was very difficult for me and the people who depended upon me. Stutterers have no place in military flying.

Fortunately, there were senior Petty Officers who were good enough to work with me. Some that come to mind were AF1 Bill Lahnen aboard the YORKTOWN and AF1 Vic Strickland who was the senior petty officer of the Memphis photo lab and the YORKTOWN lab until he was transferred to another ship. AFC Bill Blair was Chief Petty Officer of the YORKTOWN photo lab and very understanding. Of course, I had to do my job properly. They could not permit any shortcomings.

The results of these situations were that I asked for and usually got jobs that sailor lives did not depend upon me. Aboard ship, my duty station was alone, aft on the catwalk beside the flight deck. There, I could use any camera that would do the job. This ranged from the Kodak 16mm Cine Special to the 35mm High Speed Mitchell motion picture cameras. For still photography, the Fairchild K-20 was perfect for fast shooting. After months of using those cameras, I became proficient with the uses and operation of all of them. I worked alone and preferred it. There were times I would take the position on the 07 level, just aft on the superstructure. From there, 90% of the flight deck could be photographically covered. That position was usually manned by one or two photographers. It was so noisy there it did not make much difference whether a person could talk or not. Most communications were done by hand signals.

It was great working up on the flight deck. Working in the daylight permitted me to know what was going on. Several times it was really enlightening. Once, we ran into a whale. The bow of the ship hit the mammal exactly in his middle. It was caught by the sharp bow of the ship. The whale showed great distress by thrashing its tail, rolling its eyes and profusely bleeding. We tried slowing the ship down, hoping the whale could work its way off. That didn't work. The ship had to be actually stopped dead in the water, and then

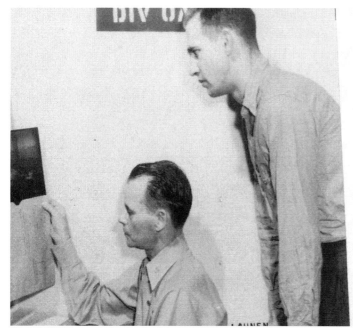

Bill Lahnen

OA Division

1952-1955

Aerial Photographer First Class Bill Lahnen looking over the shoulder of Chief Warrant Officer Photographer Mr. B.C. Abel.

backed down to permit the ship to pull out and away from the whale.

Another time, I saw something flit above the water. I had heard of flying fish but thought that was just a sea story. By keeping a eye seaward, every once in awhile I would actually see a two foot long blue fish with outstretched translucent, wing-like fins come out of the crest of a wave, sail through the air into another wave! It was amazing to see this happen. The added bonus was, the sunsets were fantastic.

Watching the big and fast aircraft take off and land on the carrier was dangerous and amazing. There were many brave men out there, in the aircraft and on the deck. With tons of aircraft coming down to the ship at 120 miles per hour, it requires a lot of precision movements to land and stop it safely. It was very difficult to accomplish this in the daylight but at night, it was very frightening.

Especially when considering these aircraft carried many gallons of aviation gasoline and various explosives.

Men were killed and others seriously hurt on the flight deck on our cruise. The flight deck of an aircraft carrier is the most dangerous place in the world to work. It certainly caused the adrenalin to flow!

After the planes were safely aboard the ship, they were pushed onto one of the three elevators and lowered onto the six inch thick armor plate of the hangar deck. There, coordinated efforts of plane directors and pushers moved the delicate aluminum aircraft into designated parking places, relative to individual squadrons. It was very important to do everything properly, down to the very last inch. The folded winged planes had to be moved carefully. They could not touch each other because it would damage the aircraft's thin aluminum skin. After properly spotting the units in place, they had to be tied down to prevent them from rolling around on the swaying deck. Those men on the hangar deck did a good job; I have never seen a plane damaged from handling.

Most of all of this was done by using hand signals. Vocal commands were almost totally absent as the other overwhelming noises would diminish the accuracy of what could be heard.

This stuttering photographer was able to do his job well, without oral communication with the working crew on the flight deck or the hangar deck. In addition to all of this, the openings on the sides of the hangar deck made good framing composition for photographs.

I enjoyed sea duty. The sea always fascinated me with the salty breezes, the flowing of the waves and swells. You never knew exactly what you might see and experience next. There were so many remarkable photo opportunities. It was especially enjoyable because it was your job to capture such scenes on film.

The Cruise Book editors loved our photographs. Sailors at work would yell at us, "HEY PHOTO, TAKE OUR PICTURE!" We would stop and do it for them. Later, we would swap those pictures to the sailors for things we needed such as food, goodies and such.

I loved the sea, the ports of call, the photography and working in and around airplanes. Serving aboard the aircraft carrier USS YORKTOWN CV-10 and with its crew was one of the greatest experiences in my long, exciting life.

Flight Deck Crew partying.

Author on flight deck duty.

Hospitalman Don Brazzon and Author.

CORPSMAN UP!!

We have all read of or seen the gallantry of the US Navy Corpsmen. Whether dispensing A.P.C. (All Purpose Capsule) at the daily Sick Call or dodging bullets to aid a downed Marine. They all do it with outstanding effort.

When non-rated Navy E3 Hospitalmen are promoted to E4, they become Hospital Corpsmen. (Those who wish to become Fleet Marine Force Corpsmen will be sent to a Marine base for special training.) Marines and sailors call them, simply, "Corpsman", "Medic" or "Doc." But when they are needed immediately, the cry is "CORPSMAN, UP!"

One day while at my camera station, aft of the ship's "island", the boiler crew (Snipes) below decks decided to blow the stacks of the ship. This is done by blowing compressed air up the smoke stacks to get rid of the soot and other dirt that may have collected there.

The black sooty particles were blown up, out and aft, down over the flight deck. I was in the direct flow of the black, greasy mess. It immediately got into my nose, windpipe and lungs. The result was I began coughing and gagging. After notifying my Leading Petty Officer AF1 Lahnen, I went to the Sickbay.

While there, due to my Pennsylvania accent, a E3 Hospitalman asked, "Are you from Pennsylvania?" I told him I was from Brownsville. He smiled and said he was from just downriver. He was raised in Belle Vernon!

While there swapping stories, I told him of my Uncle Johnnie who had been an Army Combat Medic in WWII. Johnnie lived near New Salem, not far from Brownsville. Don and I became friends.

Hospitalman Brazzon was a tall, quiet guy who enjoyed his job and liked the Yorktown. He was a good liberty buddy because he avoided trouble while enjoying visiting and learning the Oriental culture. I had similar desires but because Don was Six foot two inches tall, he was a good person to have

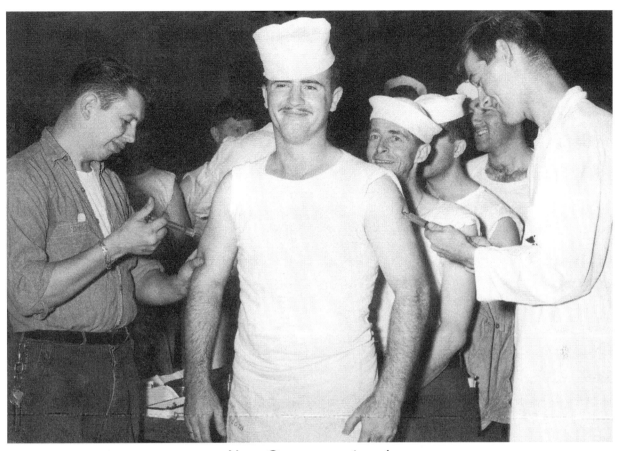

Navy Corpsmen at work.

around if we got into a bad situation. Hence, we pulled Liberty in several great ports like San Francisco, Vancouver, Canada and Hong Kong, China.

In the sick bay, when there was an emergency, HN Brazzon was a great help. For example, one day on the flight deck, the big powerful multi piston engines blew a sailor backwards and into the whirling propeller of a running engine. The sailor was badly hurt and rushed to the ships hospital by the Flight Deck Corpsmen.

Most of the damage to the man was his skull. The wound was potentially fatal. Everyone in the hospital did their best to help the doctors perform a needed miracle. Everyone who knew of the accident was very concerned. Don was called on to help in the surgery. The man was saved by the doctors who replaced the severely damaged portion of the skull with a stainless steel plate. The sailor survived.

Another instance was when Lt. Arnicar, was taking off from the ship with an Anti-Submarine AD Skyraider. The engine stopped just as the plane cleared the bow of the ship. Lt. Arnicar was rescued from the cold water, but he had a broken back and some terrible cuts. He needed an immediate blood transfusion. Hospitalman Brazzon had the same type of blood. The hospital staff put Don on another gurney, next to the stricken pilot and ran tubing from Don to Arnicar. Don's lifesaving blood flowed through the tube and directly into the aviator. Lt. Arnicar's life was saved. He was then transferred to another ship that took him to a bigger hospital in Japan. I received a phone call from Lt. Arnicar's daughter a few years ago. He is still in a wheelchair but is living a good life as an Aeronautical Engineer for an aircraft manufacturer.

On record are several times when an enlisted Hospital Corpsman, has done emergency surgery while at sea. Always under much less than ideal conditions. When a doctor is available only by radio, step by step instructions can be given, but it has occurred when no help at all was available. It takes intestinal fortitude to cut a man open when you are not a doctor, without training in surgery or proper equipment.

Fleet Marine Force (FMF) Corpsmen with the Marines do a fantastic job, but we cannot forget the dedicated Hospitalmen and Corpsmen on board the many ships that are also depended upon in life and death situations.

The Hospital Corpsman Pledge,
"I solemnly pledge myself before God and these witnesses to practice faithfully all of my duties as a member of the Hospital Corps. I hold the care of the sick and injured to be a privilege and sacred trust and will assist the Medical Officer with loyalty and honesty. I will not knowingly permit harm to come to any patient. I will not partake of nor administer any unauthorized medication. I will hold all personal matter pertaining to the private lives of patients in strict confidence. I dedicate my heart, mind and strength in the work before me. I shall do all within my power to show in myself an example of all that is honorable and good throughout my naval career."

There have been 22 Corpsmen who have received the Medal of Honor. The Navy Cross 174, Silver Star, 946 and Bronze Star 1,582. Many were posthumously.

Corpsman is the largest rate in the United States Navy.

When the flag was raised on Iwo Jima, a Corpsman helped raise it.

In the military, there are many brave men who do their duty every day and give everything they can. Most are unrecognized. But, they are there, dodging bullets, stopping blood from flowing from a wound and sewing up live flesh.

Every man who puts his life in the hands of a US Navy or US Marine Corpsman will get the best of care that can possibly be given in that situation.

Author at a party in Yokosuka, japan.

ONE DAY IN YOKOSUKA

On a Spring morning in 1954, I went ashore to shop in Yokosuka.. Usually we sailors go ashore in the late afternoon, but with my work caught up, Chief Blair let me go.

This trip was on a whim so I was not looking to purchase anything in particular. Just window shopping. The sun had dried the streets enough to tempt the local people to do the same. Because "people watching" is one of my favorite pastimes, this was like hitting the jackpot.

The old people were out enjoying the sunshine and the little Japanese kids were running about. Most of them ignored this American sailor in uniform. With my Argus C3 camera, there were many opportunities for photos. I was using black and white film because it was cheaper and I could process it in our Photo Lab aboard ship. We were permitted to do that as training exercises. When we navy photographers had to do one facet of photography for months on end, it was good to be able to take our own photos and completely process them.

There were little twin girls dressed alike at a train station, a very old man with a long beard plodding along, young ladies in kimonos leisurely strolling, a little girl dressed in red, eating raisins from a tiny red box. What a great day for photography!

Then I noticed something unusual. There was a Japanese lady going into most of the shops. She would stay a short while and then go to the next shop. I watched her until my curiosity got the best of me. As she came out of one of the stores, I walked up to her and said, in American, "How are you today?" (I hid my speech problem.)

She stopped, looked at me for a long moment and curiously answered, "I am good. And you?" After telling her about enjoying the day, city and the people, she loosened up and asked "American sailor, why you want to know?" I told her that the culture interested me.

"You like Japan?" she inquired. This opened the door to further conversation. She was appraising me and I was curious of her. Her knowledge of American sailors was limited to seeing them spending money and in general, having a good time. She never met one who was interested in Japanese culture. At that time, I knew very little of Japanese women except for the "business girls" of Yokosuka.

As we talked, I found she was a very intelligent woman with a great sense of humor. She was widowed by the war. Her husband, a sailor, had been killed in the Battle of The Philippine Sea.

Life was difficult for her because she had to support herself by being a sales lady for a supply company of cleaning goods to the businesses. She appeared to be a few years older than I. She had a different kind of grace than American women but thought a lot like them. I then asked if she was hungry, as most post war Japanese always were. She shyly admitted she was. I asked if she would like to have lunch with me. Again, she smiled and nodded her head. She led me to a little place that I had not noticed. We went through the beaded curtains and sat at a small table.

Our conversation varied from the culture, to her life and to the nice places to visit in the area. After telling her that I was a photographer, her face lit up and she asked if I wanted to see "Things to take picture?" The decision made there changed my life.

During our talk, I asked her name. She said, "You no can say. Call me Ko." But her pronunciation of Richard was not too good, either. It came out "Reechard." She asked when trying to pronounce it, "You REECH ! Ne?". I thought it was funny.

She mentioned Kamakura. That was something I had never heard of before. It was the worldwide capital of the Buddhist religion. Someplace as the Vatican is to the Catholics. My enthusiasm evidently showed because she asked, "You want go see?"

Ko and I arranged to meet the next day.

Chief Blair was knowledgeable about affairs in foreign countries. He actually understood more than I did and the next day, let me go to town with a Special Liberty.

When we met, she was all smiles and carrying a small overnight bag. I asked about the bag and she explained "Kamakura long way. Must go by train." Oh, oh, I was not prepared for that. I explained I did not know it was far away. I had not prepared. She replied, "OK, you go back ship, get days off." We talked awhile until I got the drift of what she was thinking. She had decided to take a few days off for us to travel around Japan and see things. At first, my thoughts were "Do I REALLY want to do this?' Then, after thinking about it, I decided it would really help me get acquainted with Japan as it really is. I would not only have a guide but also someone to haggle prices! The only thing that I could not figure out is how I would handle our relationship together. She was a nice lady and older than me. I wanted to remain a gentleman in order not to offend her. I did not say anything that would give her any wrong impressions.

Chief Blair again understood. He gave me a three day Special Liberty. As I left the ship, the Officer of the Deck looked into my bag and said, "Good Luck, Sailor!"

First of all, we had to take a train journey. I had seen Japanese electric trains from afar. They were very fast. After Ko bought the tickets, we waited in a crowd for the train to arrive. Ko told me, "When doors open, run in!" The train stopped and opened the doors. There was such a rush of people trying to get into the train we were swept along with the crowd. We got in but there were still people on the landing. They kept squeezing into the overcrowded car. There were uniformed men on the landing that were actually pushing more people into the car. It began to be very uncomfortable.

Fortunately, Japanese do not have body odors due to taking their wonderful daily baths. Otherwise, it would have been decidedly more unpleasant. After the train went a few miles out of the city and more and more people got off, the train car became comfortable.

We progressed through the countryside of rice paddies, gardens and trimmed fruit trees with many scenic views. Then, the train stopped at a station that was seemingly in the middle of nowhere. There was a large building nearby. Then, a door at the station opened and a swarm of elementary and junior high students swarmed toward the train. They were all girls and dressed in uniform. The big building was a girl's school that had dismissed the students for the day. I didn't expect what I saw.

Every one of those girls was dressed similar to my US Navy uniform. They each had on a dress blue jumper with white piping around the cuffs and the collar that fell down over the back of their shoulders. There were even the white stars! They each had on a white hat exactly like the one I was wearing and had shiny black shoes! However, they were not wearing slacks but had on matching dark blue skirts and white knee high socks. I was shocked, to say the least. That astonishment was mutual. They evidentially had never seen an American sailor in dress blues.

When Japanese girls giggle, they hold a hand over their mouth. IMMEDIATELY many little golden hands went over mouths and the noisy giggling soon filled the train car. There must have been fifty little girls from six years to about 10 years old and all of them giggling and pointing at me! Even Ko had a wide smile and was enjoying every second of it. Surely, my face was red in embarrassment. Then, beginning to see the humor in the situation, I smiled and waved to them. They were all around me. Those dark shining eyes laughing so much, some had tears running down their cheeks!

After the girls, Ko and I settled down and accepted the situation, we began to smile at each other. In a short time, the train stopped again to permit the girls to get off. As it stopped and the doors opened, the girls took one last look at me. I came to attention and saluted them. As one, they all snapped to attention and returned the salute and then ran off, giggling. Ko was smiling at me.

We departed the train at Kamakura. It would be a lifetime of remembrances. Ko said we must get a place to stay for the night, before the crowds arrived. We went to a little inn, went to the counter, the clerk came up and I held up two fingers. Ko signed the register and after a haggle about the price, I paid. We received two keys. As we went to the rooms, Ko asked, "Why two rooms?" I said "I respect you as a lady and want you to have good things." She was obviously surprised and disappointed, but tried to hide it.

We visited Kamakura. The guide was very helpful and spoke perfect English. He said the red paint was over 300 years old and showed us things that I considered purely mythical. There was a very large Buddha outside. It had to be forty feet tall. We were led around to the back of it where there was a door. After going inside, the story was told about now that we were inside we had the soul of the Buddha. It was very unusual as this was the original Buddha that all others were the imitation of. Next was the bridge. If you have ever seen a Japanese garden, you will find a bridge. The bridge walkway is semi circular. It is at an angle that is impossible for the human foot to cross the bridge without turning the foot sideways. It is because the foot does not bend enough at the ankle. Their faith tells them that if a person can walk across this bridge, without turning their foot sideways, he is a God.

In the area were several Japanese ladies in kimonos and most of them had children. They each had bags of what appeared to be popcorn. They would scatter it around and droves of pigeons would flock to squabble over it. The little kids, who were also in costume, were having a great time feeding the hungry birds.

By then, it was getting late. We needed to have dinner, baths and retire for the night.

The meal was simple but filling. The steaming rice had bits of chicken and the tea was hot. Ko and I enjoyed talking about the train ride with the little girls, the history of Kamakura and the meal. We had a bit of warm sake and enjoyed each other's company.

It was time for bathing. The bathroom was very spacious with one large ceramic tub. In Japan, communal baths were common. A young lady came in and scrubbed my whole body with what seemed to be a rough brick. She did this while often dousing me with steaming water from a nearby tap. When she felt I was clean, she motioned for me to get into the tub. There were other men already there. Halfway across the tub was a white curtain. We men were on one side and the women were on the other side. When only one family would be bathing, the curtain would be opened when a single family members would all bathe together.

After the bath, with only a white robe around me, I decided to sit on the veranda in the enjoyable night air. Relaxed in my wonderment of the day's activities, I became aware that Ko had come out of her adjoining room in her white robe and sat very close to me. As we talked, she mentioned a short walk. It seemed like a perfect evening to do so. There were geta (slippers) nearby, we slipped them on our feet and left the porch. We strolled through the beautiful garden, admiring the design of it. Ko explained the symbolism of each plant, flower and ceramic pot or lantern. When we were on the far side of the garden, it began to sprinkle that turned into a gentle rain.

We had been discussing the differences between Japanese and American men. Ko complained that Japanese men were hardly ever at home and the wives were hardly ever outside of the home. The women were treated very badly while the men went to parties almost every night. Ko said she would never marry again and be subjected to such treatment.

As we were in the beautiful garden, the gentle rain continued. I love the rain; it is part of my heritage to appreciate it. We paused and I leaned her back against the trunk of a wet tree. She was surprised; her eyes showed me her happiness. I kissed her, she responded. I kissed her again and again. All over her wet lips, chin, cheeks, eyes, nose and neck and whatever of her she exposed. We stayed there, in the rain, kissing and loving each other. She was so precious, with the rainwater running down her smiling face.

She would pucker up for more kisses. There was a soft light from a nearby lantern, illuminating just us, pausing in a beautiful garden, on a warm, rainy night, enjoying each other.

On the way back to the dry veranda, she told me about the lack of romance in Japanese wives' life. It seemed odd to me how any man, Japanese or not, could possibly resist loving such a wonderful woman.

The next morning, Ko haggled with the clerk and received a refund on her unused room.

On the way back to Yokosuka, we sat next to each other, enjoying each others' touch and being close. I appreciated her very much. To me she was the epitome of Japanese womanhood. I respected her and she said it was one of the best days of her life.

We talked quite a bit on the way home. Past the manicured little farms, the girls school and enjoyed the ride.

When we returned to Yokosuka, we said goodbye, wished the best for each other and parted with some very good memories that we both knew would not be repeated.

FLIGHT DECK FUN

Working on the flight deck of an active aircraft carrier is hard. It involves long hours, hot and cold weather, handling of live explosives, high octane gasoline, around loud jet and reciprocating engines, limited hearing of orders, laborious duties, very dirty and dangerous.

A bit of fun can be excused by the officers if it does put anyone or Navy property to damage or risk. These reasons permit latitude of fun by young sailors.

When running out of fresh water, showering was limited. This is a definite problem when men live very closely, as aboard ship. Sailors tend to solve problems that affect them.

On one occasion, when showers were off limits, the ship ran into a rain squall. Many of the flight deck men were very wet. Someone produced a few bars of soap and handed them out, thinking the lads would wash their faces and hands. However, they did not stop there. Soon the caps and jerseys were off and tossed on the deck. Major soaping was being done. Next to be pulled off were the socks and boots. Men were grinning and motioning for the next and final step. They took off their trousers and soaped themselves completely. Then the unthinkable happened!

The ship ran out of the rain squall into bright warm sunshine. Clothes were put back on the soapy bodies. For the rest of the day, many members of the flight deck crew walked funny and scratched a lot.

There was another trick those hard working deck hands liked to do. The opportunity arose on October 23, 1953.

Lt. Lattin of the USS ORISKANY CVA 34 needed to make an emergency landing. The only ship available was the USS YORKTOWN CVA 10. He made a safe landing. The event was a cause of merriment on the USS YORKTOWN but resulted in some grief aboard the USS ORISKANY because the crew of the USS YORKTOWN, in the spirit of Navy tradition wrote all over Lt. Lattins' Cougar jet!

The beautiful, latest model of the Grumman fighter planes had written all over it   many notes and names for the USS ORISKANY crew to wash off. . Of course, only chalk was used to facilitate cleaning.

Several other times, planes from other carriers had to land aboard the CVA 10 during our cruise and were duly used as messengers to it's parent ship.

Only one time, in 14 months, did a Yorktown aircraft return in that condition!

POOPY-SAN

During one of our calls at the Japanese port of Yokosuka, barges with two unfamiliar aircraft aboard them pulled along side. These were very large twin rotary engine planes with big four bladed propellers. The strange looking aircraft were loaded aboard the USS YORKTOWNS' flight deck. There also appeared to be another strange thing. It appeared to have a jet engine exhaust below the tail.

The AJ airplanes were numbered #2 and #4. Plane #2 had "Poopy-San" (Translation: Mr. Poopy.) printed right below and on the side of the pilots' position. Plane #4 had "Ichi Ban" (Translation: Number One.) printed on it.

They appeared too large to take off from our flight deck, especially by using our underpowered hydraulic catapults. We thought they were put aboard to be transferred to some Naval Air Station. However, attracting attention were the fold down vertical stabilizers and the ability to fold their wings. Why would a land based aircraft need to be folded up for storage aboard ship? The odd planes were stored on the semi hidden hangar deck. Additionally, who ever saw a airplane with rotary engines AND a jet? Sections of these planes were covered with tarps, as if to hide something.

At sea, three days later, these two large planes were uncovered and moved up to the Flight Deck. We flight deck photographers were full of questions.

They were moved to the forward end of the flight deck and prepared for takeoff! We had no specific orders concerning photographing these very large planes. But, as the flight deck operations were within our scope of responsibility, we began to take photos.

The heavy planes were worked into positions on the catapults and the catapult Officer gave the directions to prepare to launch one at a time.

As #2 Poopy-San turned up the motors full power, the single jet engine beneath the tail began to scream, the Catapult Officer gave the signal to launch. The monster began its move by catapult and its own power. It appeared impossible for it to achieve airspeed by the time it reached the forward end of the flight deck.

The seemingly lumbering, big and heavy plane reached the end of its assisted launch and went over the bow. It dipped down toward the water; all of us were holding our breath. It seemed it would plow right into the next swell. But, it did not. With all three engines screaming, the plane recovered and began to gain altitude. It then disappeared into the clouds. We all breathed sighs of relief. Plane #4 Ichi Ban was then successfully launched.

My curiosity was worked up to a high fever. WHAT were these big three engined airplanes? I noticed the Plane Captain of POOPY SAN seemed to have a minute. After trying to get some answers from him, I invited him down to the photo lab for a cup of coffee. He gratefully accepted.

In the Photo Lab, I whispered to Aerial Photographer First Class Bill Lahnen that I needed him to have a coffee with the Plane Captain and I.

After we three were comfortable, I explained to the Plane Captain that I needed the information about the plane to caption the photographs. Naturally, I was cleared for SECRET and the information would be restricted. He hesitated, but AF1 Lahnen interrupted and agreed with me that the information we had would only be used properly. The Plane Captain was relieved and the coffee (With a bit of "something extra.") in it was working. He began to talk.

The planes were AJ's. They were designed to carry Atomic Bombs long distances after being launched from aircraft carriers. (Maybe the story of Billy Mitchell influenced some aircraft designer.) The AJ carried a crew of three and was lightly armored. It was fast enough to outrun potential interceptors.

The planes were powered by a pair of Pratt & Whitney R-2800 Double Wasp radials and an auxiliary Allison J33 Turbojet in the lower rear fuselage.

The jet engine was intended to provide a high speed "dash" capability during the attack phase and for carrier take off.

AJ Poopy San ready to launch from flight deck.

The Plane Captain finished his coffee, excused himself and went back topside. Lahnen and I were satisfied. Of course, we cleared all information with our Photo Officer, CWO4 Abel before we wrote any captions for the photos.

The AJ's were gone for several hours. They were probably burning fuel to make them lighter and less prone to catching fire if they had an unfortunate accident while landing. When they returned to the area of the ship and into the landing pattern, we again were skeptical. After all, the arresting cables have been known to snap in two when much lighter and smaller planes landed! A broken cable flying whip-like through the air is a killer. If it hit a person, they were dead. (It had happened a month earlier.)

As AJ #4 made an unremarkable landing and taxied forward to its parking position, the nylon barriers were raised again. We were expecting AJ #2 "Poopy-San" to make a comparable landing.

It made a proper approach to the ship, the Landing Signal Officer giving #2

Poopy-San the proper directions to come right above the deck. He then gave the signal to "cut the engines" and drop that big airplane onto the deck at about 120 miles per hour. The bulky plane did exactly that.

The tail hook caught cable #3 perfectly, the big plane stopped. At that point in time, a loud metallic "CRRAACK" and the unmistakable chopping noise caused by a BIG propeller tearing up the wooden flight deck! It was heard by all hands on the flight deck! We all looked at the plane! The left big radial engine was rapidly dropping down from the wing! We were all aghast! The big engine stayed attached to the wing, but was pointed down to about a 30 degrees angle! In Naval Aviation, this was UNHEARD OF! The mountings of the engine to the wing had broken!

The crash crew ran over to appraise the situation. There was no fire, hence CWO4 Boats'n Lenz, who was in charge of the flight deck, decided not to put fire foam on the engine. The four bladed prop was badly bent from chewing up the wooden flight deck.

The expression on the AJ pilots faces were beyond description! Eyes resembled saucers; their mouths were open enough to see both pilots' sets of teeth! What if the engine mountings would have failed in flight! What if.......?

At that moment, some flight deck crewman said, "Poopy-san sure made two pilots and a crewman claim the name!"

The "Experts" aboard the ship appraised the engine as not having been designed with proper support.

When the pilots of the ill fated AJ #2 "Poopy-San" were seen on the ship, they were met with a wide grin by the enlisted men. The officers of the Ships Company, as they would make eye contact, would comment with "Good Day, Poopy-PANTS!"

After retuning to Yokosuka, both AJ's were reloaded back onto barges and towed away in disgrace to some secret hiding place.

The ship's laundry had needed to wash and bleach three flight suits....twice.

INTER SERVICE ANIMOSITY

We sometimes wonder why one branch of our military does not like the other. Is it because we are different? Believe in different things? Compete for the same women, bars or whatever?

Maybe it is just generated because some little person wants to be big.

When we would visit a port, foreign or Stateside, I would enjoy good liberty. It seemed counter productive to get into trouble when the time that was available to enjoy the port was short lived before we would go to sea again. .

To get ashore without money was not enjoyable. To get in town and still have adventure, I would volunteer for Shore Patrol duty. Sometimes that got quite exciting.

In 1953, we were tied up in Sasebo Japan. I was broke again, so I volunteered for the duty. I was instructed to report to the Shore Patrol/Military Police station that was located at the Fleet Landing.

At the appointed time, I showed up to walk into what was, at one time, a police station and sort of a Night Court. It was equipped with benches and up front was a six foot high desk. On each side of the desk was a column with a big glass ball on each of two stands. Sitting behind this enormous desk was a little US Marine E3 corporal. He was the shortest Marine I had ever seen, but with the big, loud mouth, combined with an obnoxious monumental ego.

He told me to sit down and snarled, if he needed me, he would tell me. Even though I outranked him, in this situation, he was THE authority.

While sitting there, two sailors from outside came into the room. The little E3 corporal asked them, "What do YOU want?" Both of the men were E4 rated sailors. One spoke up and said, "Something is suspicious. We think there is a spy out there!" The corporal gruffly asked, "What makes you think THAT?" "Well, some Jap guy at a shop kept asking us what ship were we from, how many men were aboard and how many airplanes we carried." The E3 Corporal said, "We will look into it. Sit down on that bench by the wall." The sailors complied.

The E3 Corporal called two E5 sailors who were Shore Patrol and told them to get the information about where that Jap civilian was and get a pick up truck and go check it out. He then turned to me and another sailor Shore Patrol beside me and told us to go with the men in the U.S. Navy truck. We went outside and got into the back of the Navy gray painted truck, in the enclosed topper, there were some seats. We rode up and down the narrow streets until we arrived at the place were the two sailors told us it was located..

At the shop was a Jap who fit the description that was given to us. We four Shore Patrolmen got out of the truck, walked up to the Japanese man. The two higher rated men asked him questions such as:

Have you been asking sailors what ship they were from? Have you been asking sailors how many men were on the ship? Have you been asking sailors how many airplanes are on their ship?

The man's normally narrow eyes opened up wide and he said, "No, me no ask funny questions about ships, men, planes. No me. Maybe someone else!"

I was aghast! What did our guys expect him to say? Did they expect a full confession? What idiocy!

We all got back into the truck and returned to the station. The two Shore Patrolmen who were in charge, told the little Corporal that the Jap did not ask questions like a spy. He had denied everything.

The Little Corporal slowly turned his head toward the two sailors who made the initial report. He scowled as he looked at them. Up and down. He then asked, "WHAT do you have in that paper bag?" One of the two sailors said, "A bottle of Akadama wine." They were then asked, "Has it been opened?" The answer was affirmative.

The little corporal stood up and yelled, "You come in here with a open bottle of alcohol, give us some bad information, we checked it out. You have not only committed a crime by bringing in that open bottle but also lying to ME! YOU caused our Shore Patrolmen to waste time looking for a SPY that does not exist!" He then yelled to a Marine that was standing in the hallway that led to two cells, "PUT THEM INTO THE FAR CELL! Bring that bottle of wine up here!"

The two E4 rated sailors were put into the cell. The little E3 Corporal then yelled to the Marine, "THEY LOOK DIRTY TO ME, GIVE THEM A BATH!" The Marine said, "YES CORPORAL!" He then unwound a fire hose that was hanging on a wall bracket, turned it toward the two unbelieving sailors and turned the hose on, FULL BLAST!

The power of the very cold water coming out of that high pressure fire hose knocked the two sailors down, into the far corner of the cell. They were doused up to their heads and down to their shoes, knocking the spit shined shoes from them and scattering them on the cement floor, their two white hats were also knocked on the dirty floor. Their skin became red from the force of the water striking them.

At that time, a tall Marine Gunnery Sergeant, with medals halfway up his chest, walked in the front door and asked the Corporal, "What is going on here?" The Corporal told the Big Gunny Sergeant the story. The Gunny listened. His face got red; the neck veins began to stand out.

The little Corporal thought the Gunny was approving of what he did to those rascally swabbies and added more while smiling from ear to ear.

While the Gunny listened to the story, he motioned to the other marine to put the hose back to onto the rack where it had been stored.

When the little Corporal finally stopped talking, the Gunny very quietly said, "Corporal, please go into my office and wait for me." The little Corporal was still smiling. Probably expecting to receive a verbal commendation, he swaggered into the office and closed the door quietly.

The Gunny told the Marine who used the hose to unlock the cell and let the sailors out. When the doused and very cold and wet sailors came out, the Gunny softly told them. "I'm very sorry this has all happened. Please accept my apology. However, I cannot give you the wine back. It is against regulations. You may leave now."

The Gunny went into his office, slammed the door and spoke to the Little Corporal. The words were loud, authoritive and in detail. Among other things we overheard "YOU WILL BE ON PERMANENT NIGHT GUARD DUTY AT THE SUPPLY DUMP!" and "YOU WILL BE REDUCED ONE RANK!" and "HOW DARE YOU DO A THING LIKE THAT!" The only thing the Corporal would say was a very low, "Yes Gunny, yes Gunny, yes Gunny, yes Gunny!"

Out in the room we were in, everyone was smiling. Even the Marine who wielded the fire hose, he didn't like the little Corporal, either!

The point is that there are bad and incompetent people in every branch of the military. But, those who cause trouble are remembered.

It reflects on the entire military group in a very negative fashion and the story gets repeated many times by sailors throughout the Fleet. Happenings like this make for bad inter service relationships.

CLEMENTINE

One of our photographers was Airman Jones. He was a seventeen year old who had signed up for a "Kiddie Cruse." That was a special enlistment the Navy offered. If a seventeen year old enlisted, he would be discharged on his 21st birthday.

Jones was blue eyed, short, slim, blond, did not yet have a beard and very young looking. He was also shy, reserved and quiet. He was also a good sailor.

While at sea, things got tiresome with the long hours every day, seven days a week. Life was dangerous, tough and boring.

 LCdr. Yeager, who was in charge of the crews' morale, decided to have an "Amateur Hour" on the Hangar Deck. There would be magic tricks, hypnotism, boxing and skits. Each Department was asked to contribute something. Our OA division was full of fertile minds and tried in vain to come up with something funny and unusual. Then, someone thought of young Airman Jones! He looked so young, pure and innocent. Hmmmm. As a young girl would be! But what would we have him DO?

We asked him to join the discussion and maybe volunteer something. After brainstorming, we all came together with an idea that Jones agreed to. It would really be "different".

 He did more than cooperate. We asked him if he knew how to act like a girl. He blushed and said, "Heck, I had four sisters. I was raised around girls, I know how they act and move." Jones stood up, sexually strolled around the compartment, and turned his head to one side, smiled and sashayed to the desk and bent over it! We were overjoyed and shocked! We had some tricks up our sleeves to add.

Airman Jones had one condition. We were not to take photographs. We agreed.

We were all sworn to secrecy.

Two of us were to write a script, another to get the make up, two others to get the dress made, Lahnen requisitioned a new swab (mop) head and talked to the Yorktown Band Leader. Our Photo Lab Chief Blair said if we had any problems to refer them to him. The hardest thing to get was a pair of saddle shoes.

It was so secret that the Photo lab door was locked when they were making props and practicing the skit. Only the people involved were allowed to know what was going on.

The night of the smoker, the #1 elevator was lowered to about four ft above the hangar deck. That would be the stage. There were so many of the crew and officers that we ran out of chairs and benches. Sailors sat on the flight deck, with their legs and feet hanging down into the elevator hole. The Yorktown Band was playing popular tunes to let people know that it would be a gala night.

The lights dimmed. Some Chief with a big nose and claiming to be a hypnotist came out and asked for a "volunteer". The "volunteer" was put in a trance and did stupid things. Two cooks said they were going to show us how the Japanese baked. After getting themselves covered with flour, singing and throwing some dough around, they pulled a pre cooked cake out of a cardboard oven. (Japanese homes did not have ovens.) A Barbershop Quartet sang a few old songs like O'SUZANNA and LUCKY OLD SUN. There were two boxing matches but nobody actually hurt anyone.

When the audience got a bit bored, the lights really went down low. A spotlight came on and lit up a door beside the elevated elevator/stage. Everyone became curious. The band began to play OH MY DARLING CLEMENTINE! The door opened and a slim, leg came through the opening. Next, as the leg came out even more, a flimsy, short, laced skirt appeared, a very pretty blonde haired, rosy cheeked Jones wiggled out. He was dressed in a short, above the knees, red and white checkered dress, pink petticoat, white sox, Navy shoes with a lot of white polish to make them into Saddle Shoes, red lips from red chalk, pink cheeks from more chalk and a head full of bright blonde hair with red ribbons! (A new mop/swab was combed out, curled with an electric soldering iron. and dyed with shark repellent yellow).

He was really cute!

On his toes, Jones slithered up four steps to get to the elevator's deck (Naturally pulling up his dress to show the slim, cream colored, hairless legs.) The GUYS WENT CRAZY! The male audience was up and yelling "WHERE DID SHE COME FROM!" Jones then went through sexual movements with the words of the song "OH MY DARLING CLEMENTINE," while the band played and a band member sang the vocals.

Naturally, Jones was spinning, twirling, swishing and wiggling all over the stage, smiling, rolling his eyes, tilting his head to one side or the other and looking very sensuous and feminine.

Sailors were standing up, whistling and stomping their feet! Jones loved the applause! He was grinning and smiling.

At the end of the song, Clementine curtsied, bowed very low and tipped her shoulders forward to display dyed flesh colored, stuffed socks she was wearing in under her low cut blouse. The girl crazy sailors went wild as he quickly skipped tip toes across the stage, throwing kisses, oozed down the steps and melted through the open doorway.

The spotlight did not turn off, as the door slowly began to close, it stopped, opened back up a little bit, Jones slowly slid a bare leg out through the door opening, all the way up his thigh, then enticingly, slowly and slowly pulled the well formed leg back out of sight to let the sex starved male sailors go absolutely crazy!

The guys sitting on the flight deck with their legs hanging down into the elevator hole were laughing and yelling so much they had to hold on to each other to prevent from falling thirty feet to the lowered elevator!

Sailors DO have fun!

Sailors sitting on the edge of #1 elevator opening to watch the show.

HONG KONG AND TIGER BALM GARDENS

As our impressive USS YORKTOWN CVA -10 picked up the Chinese Harbor Pilot (He came out to meet us in a small boat, came aboard to guide our ship into the harbor and advise us how to tie up to the buoy.) then slowly ply through the still, clean, gray and smooth waters of Hong Kong Bay, it seemed that most of our Ships Company and Squadron members were lined up at the side rails.

The city was located on an island just off the Chinese Coast in the South China Sea. We had been at sea for a month and through a terrible typhoon. Both the ship and the crew needed a well deserved rest. Our crew was anticipating five days in the fabled port of Hong Kong.

The USS YORKTOWN had never before visited the British Crown Colony. Britain had operated the colony from the turn of the 20th Century and would continue to do so until the year 2000. That year, it would be signed back to China. The Chinese businessmen of the city welcomed this because it attracted shipping, tourism, shopping and military ships from all over the world. (Chinese have many "different" ways of making money.)

This Harbor was unique because it contained thousands of "Boat People". Most of the little 12 ft boats were the home of complete families, from babies and parents to grandparents. Some of the boats had cages for chickens. The decks were flat with the top of the gunwales. Under the decks was storage for all of the family possessions.

As Mt. Victoria on the left dramatically came into view, the very prim and modern Kowloon, the city across the bay, gloriously became visible on the right. The crew had been informed that Kowloon was off limits to us. Then, the magnificence of the fabled HONG KONG, "Pearl of the Orient" became exposed on the port (left) side of the ship. The more we saw of it, the more impressed we became.

After the fabled Mt. Victoria became in full view, the city became more enticing. While rounding the curve in the channel, we saw the newer part of the city with its tall Western style buildings, the tops of the shops and the signs beckoning to sea faring men.

The biggest and most obvious sign was the gigantic billboard with a BIG blue star on a white background. It invited us to visit the Blue Star Tailors. As we progressed around the turn, the old part of Hong Kong became visible. It looked like any other war torn Oriental city. Very run down with damaged buildings, Chinese characters painted on them and dangerous looking. Unfortunately, the Fleet Landing was there. Fleet Landing is where the liberty boats from the ships would dock to expel the anxious sailors. From there, we would need to get into the major, new part of the city where the British trained Chinese police were in force and ruled that part of the city with an iron fist in a gloved hand for sailors but very tough on the Chinese residents.

It was all very impressive and exciting to my buddy Don Brazzon and I. Don and I had become friends after we found that we were raised very close to each other along the Monongahela River in Southwestern Pennsylvania. Don was much taller than I. He was six feet two inches. We both had the accent of SW Pennsylvania and loved those old hills. He worked in the ship's Sick Bay as a medic.

Don and I had already pulled some great liberties together in San Diego, San Francisco, Seattle and Vancouver, Canada. We seemed to have a mutual enjoyment of similar activities. After almost getting into trouble several times, we now had enough experience to stay out of problem situations.

After the ship was tied to the assigned buoys in the harbor, a sleek, white, civilian, fifty foot yacht came close. As our Gangway was lowered, the craft came alongside. A uniformed Chinese came out of the bridge of the beautiful boat and with a megaphone, called to our Officer of the Deck to ask permission for a Chinese National to board the USS YORKTOWN. Permission was granted. Many of our crew had lined the rail to admire the design of the yacht.

Then, we all got a big surprise!

Hong Kong Harbor.

The stern deck of the white boat was enclosed by a luxurious dark, long green felt drape, trimmed with gold Chinese characters. As we watched, a slit in the drape opened up. Through that opening came a slim, perfectly formed female ankle and calf. Then, the thigh came through, showing a long black Chinese dress with a slit all the way up the side of it. The slit extended to the upper thigh! The rest of the lady appeared. She was absolutely beautiful! Tall, slim, jet black hair rolled into a tight bun and with the biggest smile any one of us remembered! The word must have been passed to the rest of the crew for it seemed like all 3100 crewmen were at that rail. We were applauding, cheering and whistling at the beauty of that mysterious lady! She appreciated the attention, smiled some more and waved to all of us! Each member of that crew felt she was waving specifically to HIM!

She walked forward, between the gunwale (The upper edge or rail of a boat's side.) and the cabin and then stepped gracefully on to platform at the bottom of our gangway. She gave her admiring crowd the sight of a teasingly perfect body.

The "oooohs" and "AHHHHHS" were respectfully given.

As she climbed the steps up the gangway, each step displayed another long look at a sensuous, slim leg.

Capt. McKecknie and other officers greeted her as she stepped aboard. The word came down to enlisted men that the lady was a representative of the Hong Kong Chamber of Commerce. She was to arrange for Chinese merchants to have a bizarre on the hangar deck for the crew for one day while the ship was in the exotic port.

The Chinese certainly knew how to get the attention of the all male crew!

After Liberty Call was piped by our Boatswain Mate, we couldn't wait to get ashore. The rides in the open motor launches were uncomfortable, but we didn't care. After all, WE were going into HONG KONG, THE PEARL OF THE ORIENT! In addition, I wanted to see Tiger Balm Gardens.

At Fleet Landing, there were many men to pull you, in rickshaws, into the city. It was only a few blocks but for the unaware, it could be dangerous. Some of our sailors had been to Hong Kong on other ships. They warned us of possible dangers. For example, you had to keep yelling to the Rickshaw Boy to stay on the main thoroughfares. They would prefer to take the alley ways where their gangs of cohorts would hide out. The Rickshaw boys would throw up the two wood bars they used to pull the vehicle. This would tip the passengers backwards onto the bricks. There, the thugs would come out and rob them. Not only would they take money but even shoes! Don and I had heard of those tricks, so we kept yelling at the boy to go the safe route we wanted to travel.

Mary Soo and her side cleaners.

After getting into the city, HARRY's restaurant was the most famous. However, eating there required some discretion.

Mary Soo and her side cleaners would clean the sides of the ships in port. Their only pay was the ships excesses of the mess halls. Mary Soo would then sell this former Navy food to famous HARRYS Restaurant who spiced it then sold it. So, you had to select food that was obviously not from ships.

After passing HARRYS, we began to walk the streets. There were many things to attract the sailors. There were a lot of custom tailor shops. They would take your measurements and show you the finest handmade suits, dinner jackets and slacks. Personally, I wanted a pair of slacks. I selected, to be made, a blue silk, a semi western style with wide belt loops and flaps over the back pockets. They measured my waist, inseam, outward seam and other measurements. They told me the slacks would cost $3.00 and to come back the next day for more fitting. I went back for two more fittings and had a beautiful pair of tailor made slacks.

Don also took advantage of the tailor shops. After being measured, the Chinese showed him a variety of materials. He selected light brown for a cashmere suit at only $10.00 and herringbone material for a sport coat for $8.00.

But, the trick used by those tailors, jewelry, watch and gem stores was when you went in, the salesman took you to a little cubicle to show you his wares. He would offer you a beer. Naturally, sailors enjoy free beer. But newcomers would not realize the beer being given them was San Miguel Beer. It was distilled in the Philippines in a brewery owned by General Douglas Macarthur. It was VERY high in alcohol. After a bottle or two of San Miguel, an unwary sailor would buy almost anything! Don and I were aware of the game and wouldn't drink any of the beer....or anything else when we were dealing with the Chinese.

We remembered other sailors telling us to visit Tiger Balm Gardens. That sounded interesting. We didn't know how to get there. We had to ask someone.

The city was full of sailors. Not only Americans from the several ships from our Seventh Fleet, but English and Aussies. We had been told not to antagonize the English sailors. They were belligerent toward American sailors. The Aussies were good natured, who liked to drink beer, sing and tell sea stories. Don and I looked till we saw a friendly looking Aussie sailor and asked him how we get to Tiger Balm Gardens. He told us how to get there but suggested we hire a guide to locate and visit the Gardens.

It was now afternoon and we really wanted to see the Gardens before dark. So we asked about a guide. The Aussie said, with a big smile, "Ye gotta go to a cathouse. There you rent a bit of fluff and she can take you roundabout. Then, you can have some fun and games, too!" He pointed out a convenient place to go to. We were strangers in town, so we went where he directed.

Tiger Balm Gardens.

141

Miss Lu, our guide.

As we crossed the street and approached a beautiful red, wooden, carved door, it suddenly opened! An American sailor came storming out.

As he cleared the doorway, he turned and yelled, "HELL, I JUST WANTED TO RENT IT, NOT BUY IT!"

No doubt the prices were very high for services rendered.

We went up to the door and softly knocked. A little window in the door opened up and a older, female, oriental face peered through. In a heavily accented voice, she asked, "You want pretty girl?" We nodded our heads and the door opened. The lady permitted us entrance.

We went inside and the Madam asked us what kind of a girl we preferred. She mentioned the different provinces of China and the characteristics of the girls from each area. As she talked, beautiful Chinese girls would walk past a open doorway. These were the girls she was describing. She informed us that we could rent a girl for a hour, the day or until the next day. She would be yours to do anything you wish. Don and I were looking at the girls and at one another.

Finally we reluctantly told the Madam we were not looking for a girl for sex. We wanted a guide to Tiger Balm Gardens. She was mystified. Why would we come to a cathouse for a guide! We explained this was our first time in Hong Kong and were ignorant in the ways of the city. Could she please help us find a girl who would be so kind as to be our guide? We would pay a fair price for this service.

The Madam looked at us like we were from another planet but then said, "I know of nice girl from nice family who needs money for college. Maybe she do this one time for you but NO funny business! If you want, I call her and maybe she come. Maybe not. We see." She went into another room, made a telephone call and then returned. She said, "I talk with Lu, she come. She nice college girl. Velly smart. Remember, NO funny business! She is RESPECTABLE girl!"

"Her family in high politics. They make trouble fo' me if you not keep what you say. Oh yes, you need pay me for what I do for you. Five dolla, 'melican!"

Five minutes later, when Lu showed up, Don and I were amazed. We had never seen such a beautiful Oriental young lady. Not only the slim Oriental figure with long dark hair and sensuous eyes in addition to a wide white smile that would stop traffic in any American city. All of this with skin perfect for a golden goddess and curves to match. She looked pure and delicate with a voice like a small tinkling fountain. Don and I were aghast! Enlisted sailors never get to meet girls like Lu.

After proper introductions, Lu suggested we get a rickshaw to take us to the Gardens. Rickshaws are designed to hold one or two persons, but with Lu between Don and I. It was a comfortable, VERY enjoyable ride. We had to pay the rickshaw boy more money because of the three of us. It was worth it.

In her soft voice, Lu explained Tiger Balm Gardens. There was a millionaire who made his money by selling a pain killing salve, a "balm". The container had a tiger printed on it. It was called Tiger Balm. He wanted to give something back to the community. In doing so, he built a beautiful symbolic garden and park for people to visit. It had intricately designed Chinese buildings. It is a place of solitude and beauty. It was good for the soul to wander through it and admire what represented the past of China.

The main group of buildings was an intricate castle. Use of marble, teak and balanced design in spaciousness was complemented by the use of sunlight, shadow and pools of clear water with big, golden fish.

Lu would explain the symbolism of the trees, water, fish, and designs of the buildings and the magnificence of the thinking needed for the construction. Some of the paintings reflected the centuries of Chinese history. It really has to be experienced to be appreciated. However, a Westerner would not understand most of it without a competent guide. Lu was very knowledgeable. She was fluent in English and very descriptive. Lu also had the ultimate respect for her heritage. It was all complemented by her class and demeanor.

After the experience of the Gardens, we asked Lu if she would like to eat with us. She very politely declined. We returned her to the house where we met. We paid her several times over the amount she had agreed to. She was very grateful. Even her way of saying "Thank You" was perfect, graceful, smiling and appreciative. Lu had class.

By then, it was dusk and Don and I wanted to visit a Pub. We found one that sounded busy and seemed to have a lot of sailors, American, English, Aussie, French and Italian. We sat at a small table and each ordered a bottle of San Miguel. As we sat and observed the different nationalities and how they acted while drinking. Someone began comparing the difference in ships.

The English ships were very beautiful. They had long sleek lines and were painted an attractive light green. Ours were bigger, boxy and painted a dull grey. Even the sailors were different. The English sailors were big and clannish; the Italians did not speak to others. The French were loud and a lot of arm waving. The Aussies were big, tanned, muscular and friendly. The American sailors drank silently, were generally of smaller stature and wise cracked between themselves.

Don and I didn't notice much of what was happening. We were sitting at our own table, minding our own business. That is when the English sailor came up to us with "a chip on his shoulder", looking for an excuse to start a fight.

The English sailor began to exclaim how much more beautiful their ships were than the American ships. Obviously he had too much to drink. At first, no American said a thing. We took it all in stride as sailor talk. Then, the English sailor got a bit close to a United States Navy First Class Boatswains Mate with hash marks halfway up his arm, he was from a Destroyer. The Boats'n, with a smile, softly replied, "They ought to be, we paid for them!"

That was what the English sailor was hoping for. He took a swing at the sitting Yank sailor, who dodged the fist, stood up and punched the drunken sailor right in the nose, breaking it. Blood went everywhere. The fight started.

The bar that Don and I had stopped in had been the scene of potential problems for the whole day.

There had been some Yorktown sailors at that particular joint for most of the day. They were drinking, dancing and flirting with the bar girls. After all, that is what sailors do on liberty.

One of the sailors had a special little dance, if you want to call it that. He was BT3 Al Larivee. He would have a bottle of beer, do some tap dancing, spin around while bending over and making other sexual movements. Then he would set the bottle of San Miguel on the dance floor, dance around it and then pick it up with his teeth, tip his head back, take a swig or two out of the bottle and then bend over and place it back on the floor. All

BT3 Al Larivee.

the time twisting, turning and gyrating in tune with the seemingly off key Chinese music. He called it "twisting". One of the songs was the ear torturing "China Night." (American sailors dubbed the song, "She ain't got no yo yo!")

As you might expect, some of the English sailors tried to duplicate what Al was doing. However, their large bulky bodies would usually end flat on their back on the floor.

The Chinese girls were yelling, "GO! GO! GO! NUMBA ONE TWISTER BOY! That would encourage Al to get more risky and gyrate even more! The girls liked American sailors because they were paid more money than the other sailors and spent and tipped generously.

Another American sailor there was a certain Yeoman First Class. He looked harmless. He had a pinkish completion, blond curly hair, a big smile and not

145

a large build. I recognized him from the Yorktown Personnel Office.

Back in San Diego, he and I struck up a friendship. One night we went to the Enlisted Men's Club. The security Shore Patrol would not permit us to enter. They said the Yeoman had the reputation of "Being the fightingest Yeoman in the US Navy."

The mix of American and English sailors, the Yeoman and 25% alcohol San Miguel beer was a recipe for trouble.

The English sailors were not only angry because the American sailor was out dancing them but also because the bar girls liked the happy go lucky American sailors than the stingy English sailors. Jealousy had built up.

Stares of "hard eyes" became more and more pronounced between the two nations' sailors in that little Chinese bar. The atmosphere was getting "frigid". Al kept right on drinking, twisting, singing and the girls loved it.

After the fight began with the English sailor and the American sailor, near us, the fight really spread throughout the bar.

A BIG English sailor yelled, "LETS GET THE YANKS, MATEYS!" Several of the English sailors rushed toward a couple of tables nearest to the bar that were occupied by American sailors.

Tables were overturned, pitchers of beer were spilled, American sailors pulled off their neckerchiefs (They were detrimental in a fight. The opposition would grab them and control the Americans by pulling the neckwear.). Some of the American neckerchiefs were loaded with rolls of dimes rolled in them for occasions like this. They would be quickly taken off and be used as blackjacks.

The First Class Yeoman jumped right into the fray. That little blond haired blue eyed guy was TOUGH. You don't expect that out of yeomen! BT3 Larivee was another one that did not shy away from a good fight. He did not look for one but you could count on him at your back! I yelled to Al and asked if he needed any help. He waved back and said, "HELL NO! GET OUT OF HERE, WELLS!"

The guidelines were to not hit someone from your own country. As far as Don and me, our guideline was to GET OUT of there! We were making it toward the door when a really big Englishman stopped us and was going to do some great bodily harm on at least one of us. Then, a really bigger Aussie got between us and yelled, "HEY BLOKE, These Yanks are ok. I know them from this afternoon. Let 'em alone! I told them how to get to a cathouse! All they wanted to do was see the Gardens!" The big Englishman stepped aside, apologized and Don and I made it outside….running. As we looked back, we could see about six Hong Kong Chinese policemen running into the bar. They would arrest people! You don't want to be arrested in CHINA! You would need an Act of Congress to get you free.

We made it back to the ship without mishap and had enough excitement for our first venture into Hong Kong.

The next time I saw BT3 Larivee, I asked him how he stayed out of the Hong Kong Jail. He smiled and said, "I got ways! The girls got me out the back door!"

Hong Kong Liberty has given me memories for all of my long life!

LOUIS ARMSTRONG vs. THE FUJI NEW GRAND

"R.G.! R.G! HEY, R.G.! Wait a minute!" Aerial Photographer First Class Bill Lahnen, Leading Petty Officer of the USS YORKTOWN Photo Lab was calling me as I was walking out the door of the Lab.

Being interrupted while on my way to noon chow made me less than a happy sailor; however, Lahnen was a good Petty Officer and treated me very well. I waited for him to catch up. He said, "I have some good news for you! You have the opportunity to see Louis Armstrong in PERSON in YOKOHAMA!"

The trip from Yokosuka to Yokohama would be by luxurious high speed electric train and a dinner in a nice restaurant. After that we were transported to the very large, ornate theater that seated thousands of Japanese. We sailors were in our Dress Blues and were ushered to reserved seats about five rows from the stage. After the introductions, Louie came out.

Louis Armstrong was one of my favorite coronet players and jazz musicians. I was immediately interested. Bill continued, "Louie will be in concert in Yokohama on New Years Eve! Do you want to go?" My answer was big smiling, "YEAH!"

He began in his style of smiling, playing his horn, telling jokes and wiping his face with a big white handkerchief. Along with the rest of the appreciative audience, I was having a time of my life.

Sitting with the band, was an attractive Rubenesque lady who was smiling a lot. Louie turned and introduced her as Velma Middleton. She was a vocalist and a dancer. Most of us had never heard of her. But, I never forgot her! She sang a tune while swirling and dancing all over the stage. It was quite an achievement for a lady of her generous proportions.

Then, she really surprised the whole theater of people by doing a SPLIT! The woman was amazing. Everyone in the theater stood up and applauded her. I never forgot that woman doing that unimaginable stunt!

Then, as she stood seductively beside Louie as he sang THAT'S MY DESIRE. Just singing was not Louis' style. He sidled up close to her, wiped off his face with the ever present handkerchief and put his lips close to her ample breasts, which were bursting out of the low cut gown. He would sing a few of the words, "...to spend one night with you, in our secluded rendezvous and dance till break of day, that's my desire...." He would roll his eyes, tilt his head and wipe his sweaty face, again and again. Velma would be singing and obviously enjoying the very close attention to her abundant figure.

Another song was equally exciting. Louis and Velma, as a duet, sang BABY IT'S COLD OUTSIDE. The tune was about his need to leave her and go home and she would sing how much he needed to stay with her. The singing, grinning, smiling, acting and reacting to the suggestive words were something to remember!

It was late when we boarded the fast train and returned to Yokosuka and the YORKTOWN; some of us were so sleepy we stumbled down to our bunks. For days, the trip was all we talked about. I never forgot AF1 Bill Lahnen for the opportunity to attend the event.

The event was very well organized and we sailors were treated very well by our guides and everybody we met. Surprisingly, the Japanese civilians were all smiles and very courteous.

The enjoyment of the Louis Armstrong Concert was such a good memory that a few weeks later when Lahnen asked who wanted to go on a Rest and Recreation trip to the mountains, this sailor from the hills of Pennsylvania was the first to jump to the occasion. Lahnen was not too happy. Our ultra conservative photo officer, ChPhot Abel, WO4 would not permit him to leave the ship overnight. He was needed aboard in case there was an emergency.

This trip was very different. On a cold, wet, January morning, there were enough sailors to fill an old, gray Navy bus. The driver was an E3 Boatswain Mate Striker who had never made the trip.

He had a problem getting the bus motor started and he ground a few gears to get it in motion. It slowly moved through the Naval Base and then into the Japanese traffic. As we left the Yokosuka area, and looking at the passing countryside, we saw many people working in well defined rice paddies, neat orchards, well taken care of neat, tiny homes and other indications of an orderly living. Riding the bumpy, cold bus as it went toward the mountains, we sailors questioned if the bus was powerful enough to make it up the angle of the grades ahead. Little did we know the steepness was minor compared to what lie ahead of us!

The driver clashed more gears. The road became more upward, narrow and curvy. The rain had increased to the point where it was difficult to determine where we were or how far we had gone. We had been miserable for hours. When would all this end?

A sailor stood up and proclaimed to be a cook. He opened a few prior unnoticed boxes and took out white bags with bologna sandwiches, passed them around along with cardboard containers of warm milk. Naturally, we sailors complained.

The driver noisily ground "another pound of gears". The creaky bus was slowly moving up the narrow road. We wiped some of the vapor from the inside of the windows. We could see a deep valley right by the road. There were no guard rails! We continued, going higher and higher into the mountains. The rain was accompanied by lightening. Water began to come in through cracks around the old, ill fitting windows. The windshield wipers were erratic vacuum operated. We were all straining to see through the windshield.

Then, all at once, we saw a very frightening, a US MARINE 6 wheeled, 2 ½ Ton Truck roaring down the narrow road and coming right toward our wide, lumbering bus! There was NO other lane for either to move to!

In unison, we sailors all screamed, yelled and cursed! There was only the little, narrow, one lane, no guard rail, a very deep valley on the right side and the left side was the mountain. It scared the bus driver so badly; he stopped the bus, right there, waiting to be crushed in the ensuing crash!

The speeding BIG truck never slowed down! Just before he would have hit our tinny bus head on, the Marine driver turned the wheels and the enormous and heavy green truck ran up on the angled mountain side of the road!

Where the road was cut out of the mountain, was a muddy, dirt, angled berm, the big green six wheeled vehicle seemed to almost turn over onto the rickety grey bus as all six wheels powered around us at a drastic degree. Those of us, who could see the heavy truck's driver, could watch that damn Marine laughing and pointing at us!

That whole bus full of sailors used language that landlubbers never heard of as they expressed their opinions of the Marine and his ancestry. After that, we became very quiet and slowly drove on.

Finally, at about 1900 hours (7pm) we pulled into the driveway of The Fuji New Grand Hotel. It was still a downpour of rain. We grabbed our little blue overnight bags and ran in. The evening meal was already over. As we were being given directions about our rooms and such, we noticed a few beautifully gowned young Japanese ladies and a band setting up in a ballroom. That began to raise our spirits. Women, booze and dancing!

An hour later, the ballroom was full of Marines, Air Force guys, sailors and more well dressed young ladies.

We soon found out there was a bit of competition with the ladies. The Marines were from the Third Marine Division encamped at Camp McNair and the Air Force guys were from some local base.

Each one of them had a girl at their table. If we wanted to dance with a lady, we would first ask the escort for permission. They would always give it. While dancing with the girls, when propositioned, the lovely's would mention they could not leave the ballroom. At first, it seemed a bit odd. However, we sailors figured it out. The Marines and Fly Boys were locals who were here every night. They knew these girls and were their regular boy friends. Naturally, they would not have a social relationship with guys who were on R&R and only be there one or two nights. They were hired to dance with everyone;

hence their escorts were obligated to give permission for them to dance with us. The drinks were very cheap, only 25 cents each. The sailors got drunk and began to fight with the Marines and Fly boys. The Military Police came in and told we sailors, fighting or not, to return to our rooms. Grumbling, we did as ordered.

When I awoke the next morning, I was SURPRISED AND SHOCKED! Lying in bed, looking out the window, the BIG and beautiful Mt. Fuji's snow capped peak took up the entire window!

It was so close; I could plainly see the little weather station in the snow at the peak! It was a magnificent sight! Without getting out of bed, reaching for my Argus C3 camera and setting focus on Infinity, I took a Kodachrome slide of the window with the mountain dominating the scene. I shall always remember that.

(If you wish to see what I am referring to, go to your search engine and type in FUJI NEW GRAND HOTEL. The entire scene is there. I cannot include it because it is copyrighted.)

It was a beautiful day; the outdoor scene from my top floor room window was breath taking. To the left was Mt. Fuji; straight out the window was the perfectly blue Lake Yamanaka. All of this was in the Fuji Hakone National Park. The grounds were perfectly manicured. A big brown and white Collie dog was sleeping on the grass, in the warm, morning sun that was drying out everything before me.

That evening, I stayed my room to get a good night sleep. We began our return trip early the next morning. Our inexperienced driver was more at ease, the box lunches were from the Hotel were much better. After the experience getting to the Hotel, going home was a much better trip. It turned out to be a tolerable experience, but none of us wanted to do it again.

Every bell bottomed, blue clad one of us was very happy to get HOME, to our beautiful, safe, secure USS YORKTOWN!

SAGA OF THE SHOWER CURTAINS

If you were to describe Steve Getz, you might say, "Good 'ol Boy." While that description would be close, it would be lacking in his description.

Getz was from Maryland. He was quiet, did his job and didn't make problems for the Petty Officers. However he had been assigned to the Photo Lab without having been through the School of Naval Photography. Without official Navy A School training, he would be utilized in positions that did not require the formal photographic schooling. That would result in being sent to Mess Cooking and/or Compartment cleaning.

Compartment Cleaning was a chore that could be done properly or haphazardly. Getz was smart enough to know that if he kept the compartment in good shape it would result in him having more time for himself.

This would result in taking the "short cuts" when doing his job.

Enlisted men's showers aboard the Yorktown did not have shower curtains. Even the most immodest sailor preferred some privacy while in the shower.

One day, shower curtains mysteriously appeared! They were white high quality canvas and did the job very well. We all thanked Airman Getz for acquiring them. When we would ask the origin of the curtains, he would just smile and say, "I have my ways." We knew not to ask any more questions. One day, after a couple of weeks of plying the waters off the United States Pacific Coast, the ship was returning to San Francisco for a few days Liberty.

When the ship tied up at Alameda, we all wanted to be showered and ready to hit the beach to enjoy the city and its vices. But, there were no shower curtains!

We found Getz and asked him what happened to the curtains. He looked concerned and said, "I'm working on it."

The shower curtains were never returned to our compartment.

A week later, while processing some aerial film that Chief Blair and AF1 Bill Lahnen took, we noticed something unusual.

There is one picture that shows the Yorktown coming into the Bay, right under the Golden Gate Bridge. Extending from the right side of the ship is a white line going down into the water. There is nothing showing of what was on the end of the line, but the angle of the line and the relationship of the angle to the speed of the ship would indicate the weight of possibly some shower curtains! We questioned Steve and here was the story he gave us.

He wanted the compartment to be shipshape for a scheduled inspection when we got into port. The shower curtains were dirty. He thought if he would hang them over the side of the ship and let them drag through the salt water, it would clean them. After all, that is how the sailors of the OLD NAVY cleaned things, by hanging them over the side. He thought he would try it, without realizing the old ships did not move through the water as fast as our USS YORKTOWN.

He tied the curtains on to one end of a sturdy line and secured the other end to the ship. After throwing the curtains over the side, he stood around for awhile but felt conspicuous standing in one spot. He left and came back a minute later to retrieve the curtains. THEY WERE GONE!

Getz said that one of several things may have happened. The line could have come loose from where it was secured to the ship, or an Officer may have seen the line and pulled it in or the original owners saw "their" shower curtains on the end of the line and re appropriated them.

The photo still exists, check and see if YOU can spot the white line.

We photo mates knew Getz would read his bible and become engrossed in it. Our opinion is that he was not telling us the whole story. We think Getz was reading his Bible in the 02 storage compartment instead of watching the curtains being pulled through the salt water and forgot how long he neglected them.

Can you find the white line?

Left to Right" Jack Kennedy, Stan Getz and two unknown men.

155

Getz spent a lot of time reading the Bible. Even though he was not a Bible Thumper, as some of his associates were, he tried very hard to live by the Holy Scriptures. However, there was one disturbing problem.

Getz loved Liberty, the kind of Liberty that sailors had the reputation of enjoying when their ship was in a port.

When he went ashore, he loved to drink, dance and celebrate. Naturally with the loose women that frequented those places, temptation for sailors was rampant, Getz would succumb to the wiles of those available women, as most sailors do.

After returning to the ship from Liberty, Getz would regret his actions. He would be very quiet and study his Bible at every opportune moment. He would be repentant.

His religious buddies would attempt to console him. But, his backsliding really bothered him.

One night I was fast asleep in my bunk. It was the top bunk of three bunks. Right across from me was another stack of three bunks. The lower bunk was suspicious. The blanket was elevated in the middle and some light was seeping through small openings. A light was on in that bunk, under the blankets! I could hear sobbing.

Getz, awake very late at night, was under his blanket, reading his Bible with a flashlight and sobbing about his transgressions!

When we went to the next Liberty port, Airman Steve Getz was one of the first sailors to rush from the ship, bound for the dens of Iniquity!

Naturally, this resulted in more late night sobbing. It was sad, but we had no alternative other than to accept him as he was. But we would not forgive him for losing our shower curtains!

HOMEWARD BOUND

After our Oriental tour of duty with Task Force 77 was completed, the USS YORKTOWN CVA 10 turned eastward, toward the Territory of Hawaii and the USA.

We recrossed the International Dateline from West to East. Warm skies, blue water, flying fish, porpoises and whales, we were finally going HOME!

When the ship reached Pearl Harbor, the wreckage of December 7, 1941 was still not cleared. There were still capsized and sunken ships in the harbor. The USS ARIZONA was mostly hidden. The only visible part of the valiant ship was a couple of slim masts above the blue-green waters of the Harbor. Bubbles of oil and air were still coming to the surface. There were Navy Divers working on many capsized or sunken ships. It was still a tragic scene, thirteen years after the Day of Infamy.

After being in the Navy for almost four years, I did not have a tattoo. This was something I had thought of. After all, how could I serve these years and go back to my hometown without some obvious symbol of my sea faring years. Don Brazzon and I talked it over and we would venture into Waikiki and get the job done. Medic Don informed me there would be some pain involved. I required some liquid fortitude.

Don and I rode the big, gray, navy bus from Ford Island into Honolulu. We saw many of the sights that were commonly discussed among sailors, the destroyed ships in the harbor, Hickum Field, the fabled Hawaiian Queen's Castle, the wide tropical avenues that led through the city. As we approached Waikiki, the pink Royal Hawaiian Hotel dominated the view. At three stories high, it was the tallest and most recognizable building on the famous beach. Arriving at Hotel Street, we left the bus and walked.

The music of the beach was truly local. The strains of "Lovely Hula Hands", the "Hawaiian Wedding Song" and other island tunes flowed from the bars and other establishments to surround and caress the ears of awe-struck visitors.

We found Don the Beachcombers thatched roof bar. It was a popular drinking establishment for sea faring men because of its outward appearance and interior décor.

Life Jackets, anchors, netting, binnacles, lines and hawsers along with paintings of mermaids and nautical artifacts hung on the walls. The booths were rumored to have been made from the wood of old sailing ships. Most of all, they employed only Hawaiians. Not just the male bartenders, but the beautiful dusky island girls as waitresses. The establishment was full of sailors and Marines who sat and drank while attempting to date the slender, dark eyed, big breasted beauties. I was still in good enough condition to take photos of one of the waitresses with my new 2 ¼ X 2 ¼ Rolleiflex camera. She had long black hair, perfect teeth and smile, friendly and beautiful. She had a commercially made lei around her neck. She was magnificent!

Don and I knew the local girls wouldn't get involved with men from the ships. They didn't want to be left behind when the vessels, after a short stay, would leave. We would only enjoy the nautical atmosphere.

After enjoying the ambience (ogling the native girls) for several hours, we were "feeling no pain". We shakily left the noted establishment with an unsteady gait and considerably fewer dollars in our tailor made white bell bottomed uniforms.

The outside salt air started our brains to function and we decided to get our bearings and rest awhile. We swayingly navigated our way to the Royal Hawaiian Hotel.

A waiter escorted us to the outside veranda. No doubt hoping the warm breezes would hasten sobriety.

He brought a list of drinks. Don and I, both still a bit fuzzy, pointed to something that contained milk. Then I sipped them and discovered a totally unusual taste. It was very good! The waiter returned with two more. Don and I were perfectly happy. We were sitting on the exclusive veranda of the grandest hotel in the Islands, sipping something very tasty. It was an exceptional, pleasurable experience.

Diamondhead volcano.

Don the Beachcombers.

159

I felt the "call to nature" and tried to rise from the chair. I promptly fell back down into it. Don laughed, and then slurred, "Wuzza matter, buddy?" I looked at him and thought, "Damn, Don is drunk. How am I goin' to get 'em back to the ship?" I again tried to rise but my legs refused to move. My little white hat had fallen to the wooden floor. I bent over to pick it up and promptly rolled down onto the deck of the veranda. My good friend began to laugh loudly, pointing at me, and gasped, "Dammit Wellsh, yer drunk as hell!" I couldn't believe what was happening. I wasn't drunk, HE was! Groggily, I asked the waiter, "Shay, what wuz in them drinks?" He smilingly replied, "Coconut milk and rum. Lots of rum." (I really do not recall if it was that or pineapple juice and lots of rum in coconut containers, but there WAS plenty of rum!) He then advised that we would no longer be served alcoholic beverages and others were waiting for the table. We had to leave the premises. While holding each other up, we swayed out on the street with other intoxicated sailors and Marines.

When drinking, my tendency to feel sorry for myself is magnified. Lately, I had been unlucky in love and it was bothering me. The alcohol made it overwhelming. As we wobbled past a tattoo parlor, I dimly recalled some bleary thing about wanting a tattoo.

Tattoos are a part of sailing men. Sailors seemed to acquire them more than girl friends or ex-wives. Many tattoos adorned the bodies of sea faring men. The tradition began when the sailing ships would be on the bounding main for years at a time. Sailors were not permitted to hold conversations, except at the water barrel, the "scuttlebutt." (The origin of the nickname for navy gossip.) One of the few things a person could do without speaking was to scribe tattoos on him or others. After many months at sea, the quantity and quality of tattoos would increase.

The skin adornments were many shapes and sizes. Some were simply names and dates of duty stations or ships. Some were favorite ports of call. Religious adornment was unusual but crosses were frequent due to the simplicity and ease of puncture. Some simple markings were the letters of H O L D F A S T on each of the four fingers of both hands, between the knuckles. The words showed when both hands were displayed. Sometimes other four letter words

160

were used, for example, T R U E   L O V E

Some tattoos were thought to be original. Most of these were only obvious when the bearer was in various stages of undress. Chests were adorned from armpit to armpit with large Clipper Ships in full sail. Sometimes a favorite modern ship was displayed with gun turrets, smoke from the stacks and colors (flags) flying. Usually the flags on ships were depicted on the breast, so when the chest muscles were flexed, the flags would appear to be waving in the breeze. Some times, hula girls would be tattooed on muscular bronzed forearms and would wiggle when the fist or fingers were manipulated.

Under or over many chest nipples were marked, "sweet" and "sour" or "white" and "chocolate". I had seen one old salt with a propeller on each cheek of his buttocks. Under the artistically drawn designs was printed "TWIN SCREWS".

Some Marines had tattoos. However, theirs were generally different. The Gung Ho types had inscriptions such as "DEATH BEFORE DISHONOR" or 'SEMPER FI MAC" (Which had a different meaning than it does now.). Many depicted the Devil Dogs with helmets and spikes on the dog collars. They were not of the same subjects as the sailors.

As Don and I staggered into the tattoo emporium, I became more depressed. I wanted a tattoo to reflect my feelings. My good friend asked, "Why do you want to mess up your body with one of those?" (He was more sober than I.) I insisted on looking at the catalogue. THERE, was what I wanted. It was a red heart, broken in two. Across the bottom was the word, "FOREVER".

I wanted that tattoo. I NEEDED that tattoo! I asked the Artiste, "How much?" He replied, "Three fifty!" That seemed reasonable to my sotted mind. He then said, with a stern look, "In ADVANCE!" He must have done a lot of business with drunken sailors. With some assistance, I crawled into the chair. Then, promptly slid down, almost to the floor. The Artiste helped Don get me back up into the chair. I asked, "Don, woulja git th' money outta ma billfold?" It was stuck into the top of my trousers. Don pulled the wallet out and looked into it and said, "There is only three bucks in here!" "What? Deres ony th'ee in dere? Couldja loan me a half a buck?" Dons' medical background guided him to say, "I don't have it to loan. I have only fifty cents to get back to the ship. Sorry, buddy."

The Artiste had seen a lot of drunken sailors, so he said, "Without the full amount, no tattoo. I have others, with money, waiting. You gotta go."

The next thing I remember it was the next morning and Don the Hospitalman was standing next to my bunk with a cup of water and two APC's (All Purpose Capsules.) He said, "Take these!"

Don told me the rest of the story.

After being told to leave, I slid down from the chair, almost to the floor. Don picked me up and put his arm down and half dragged me to a bus stop. I lay on the bench, asleep till the bus came. Don half carried me on the bus as I was 90% asleep. On the bus, I laid down again. As we went through the main gate at the base, Don got me up to a sitting position so the guard wouldn't arrest me for being drunk. He somehow got me to my bunk and into it. I don't recall any of that. Somehow, the new leather case on my Rollei was quite scratched and marred.

Don was a good friend to have. He was much taller than I was and knew what to do when a person was incapacitated. He really helped his "little buddy," when I needed a friend.

Later in the morning, sober and talking to Chief Photographer Blair, I told him of the almost inscription. The Chief sternly informed me that tattooing was against a Navy regulation that states, "Mutilation of Government property will NOT be tolerated. And, Photographers Mate Third Class Wells, YOU ARE GOVERNMENT PROPERTY!"

There were some fond memories of the "Islands" that are still with me. The beautiful Waikiki Beach, Hotel Street, the Punch Bowl, the beautiful Hawaiian women, Diamondhead, the beautiful music, swaying hula girls and the sunsets of Hawai'i. And, of course, RUM!

The next big excitement for me on the voyage back to the Good 'ole USA was the first stateside radio station we picked up. The song was played on the Public Address system and sung by Dean Martin was the first time I ever heard, "WHEN THE MOON HITS YOUR EYE LIKE A BIG PIZZA PIE, THAT'S AMORE"

When a ship approaches the San Francisco Bay, there is a noticeable difference in the sea. A peculiar swell is right off the Bay entrance. The motion of the ship in this area was a slow roll from side to side. At that moment, I was in the film developing space getting it shipshape for inspection by our CWO4, Mr. Able. There was a clipboard hanging on the bulkhead with a eight inch piece of string holding a pencil. The swaying back and forth, back and forth, back and forth of the pencil that kept catching my eye made my stomach a bit queasy. It was the ONLY time aboard ship that I ever felt any discomfort by the sea. I immediately went to Fueling Station #2, right outside the photo lab door, for some fresh air.

At that time of my life, I was undecided as to whether I should stay in the Navy or get discharged and go back home. My parents and I had been writing and Dad said he could get me a job on the outside of Clyde #1 coal mine in Fredricktown, Pa. The pay would be good and not dangerous.

It was hard to make up my mind because I enjoyed sea duty. Imagine, traveling all over the world and actually having your HOME right there with you. Or, I could be transferred to a squadron and be able to fly again! Every thing looked good!

All my life I wanted to "see the other side of the mountain" and here, I was doing it and getting paid, too! It wouldn't have been too long until I could regain my lost rate of AF2 and make good money.

I enjoyed the excitement of the Navy, but missed my family.

I was honorably discharged from the U. S. Navy on May 25, 1954

After a couple of days at home, I noticed my Dad had not gone to work. For the first week, I didn't say anything. On the second week, I asked, "Dad, are you on vacation? You are not going to work."

Dad looked at me, put his head down and said in a low voice, "Son, I lied to you. I don't have a job anymore. I can't get you a job. I didn't say anything because I didn't want you to stay in the Navy."

Dad never before lied to me. So this was something very unusual. Naturally, the shock was a great disappointment. I had spent my mustering out money on a nice yellow Chevrolet Convertible and was enjoying life on the 52/20 club. (The government paid a returning veteran

twenty dollar a week for fifty two weeks.) My uncle Jerry told me not to worry. He worked at Ford Motor Company in Dearborn, Michigan. We would go there and I would get a job in Michigan. The die was cast. I would not return to the Navy, I would go North to Land of Opportunity and get a good job.

I have always regretted my decision to not return to the US Navy. It was a good place for a single man but with my speech problem; it would be tough to find a good navy wife.

After two months working as a photographer in Dearborn, the Ternstedt Division of General Motors hired me. I retired 33 years later as a Quality Control Engineer. (During this time period, I enlisted in the US Marines as a RECON Squad leader for three years.)

I still have the photo that I took of the beautiful Hawaiian waitress at Don the Beachcombers! It keeps my memories of "the Islands" fresh!

The author as Sgt. of Marines.

RICHARD G. WELLS, MARINE!

Many people have asked me, "Why did you go from the Navy to the Marines?"

The answers are in my youth.

Good men taught me proper shooting techniques. When I was about twelve years old, Pip Caglia and his friends would buy a box of .22 cartridges. We all would go to a place safe to share and to shoot.

The Boy Scouts taught interesting skills. Woodcraft, living in the woods, the constellations in the night skies, making meals of what is available, observation, map reading and mapmaking, using basic tools to build shelters, animal life, being independent and most of all, survival in adverse conditions. And importantly, honor and respect God, Country and Family.

In 1950, when I decided to serve our Country and had my bag packed to go to Uniontown, Pa to enlist in the US Marines, my Mother noticed a little USMC emblem on my bag. She stopped washing clothes, looked me straight in the eyes and said, "Son, please do not enlist in the Marines." I obeyed my mother and joined the Navy. I have enjoyed and appreciate what the US Navy helped me accomplish.

After my four years in the US Navy and observing marines, my desire to become one of them grew stronger. Back as a civilian, the call was still within me, the Brotherhood of the Corps was still beckoning. I could not resist.

Because of my Scouting and Navy backgrounds, the US Marines restored my E4 rank to Sergeant and RECON Squad Leader.

It was a good three years. The Brotherhood of the Beloved Corps continues with me to this day.

Proudly, I still proclaim, "After fifty years, I am still a MARINE!"

WHY THE MARINES ARE THE OLDEST CONTINUAL UNITED STATES MILITARY SERVICE

• All Marines know they are the longest continual military service in the United States of America.

• The Corps has participated in every war the United States has been in and has taken part in more than 300 landings on foreign soil.

• In 1738, the British Government asked the colonists to supply 3,000 Marines to fight in the War of Jenkins Ear in the West Indies. Only 10% survived!

• Marines are for the express purpose of fighting, as opposed to those who actually navigate and sail the ships. In addition, they may be called on for Mess or Sideboy Duties.

• On July 10, 1775, Congress decided to raise two battalions of Marines, at Congressional expense.

• Recruiters, along with fifers and drummers "drummed up" the first enlistees for the Continental Marines. The drums, emblazoned with coiled rattlesnakes and the motto, "DON'T TREAD ON ME!" caught the attention of Benjamin Franklin and later the design was used on the first American Battle Flag. (In the year 2010, it was used on the "Tea Party" flags.)

• From 1775 to 1783 these drummers and fifers served afloat and participated in the naval engagements of the Revolution. They also served ashore with the Army at the battles of Trenton, Princeton and Penobscot Bay.

• In 1783, When the Revolution ended, Congress disbanded ALL US Military services. However, some Marine drummers and fifers were retained on duty and served on a few State vessels.

• When the United States Navy was re-born in 1797, with the launching of three frigates, Marine fifers and drummers served on them. At that time, the rest of the US Military was reactivated, along with the rest of the Corps.

• This is how the Marines became the longest continual serving U.S. Military… because of a few drummers and fifers serving aboard the various State owned vessels from 1783 to 1797.

References: The MARINES, Marine Corps Heritage Foundation David Schwalbe, The Birth of the United States Marine Corps

NON-TYPICAL MARINES

The stories in this chapter are of two Marines who needed to be advised of the correct way to do things. I really do not want to write these, except if you read them with a sense of humor.

When a man enlists in the Beloved Corps, he shows a great bravery in doing that. He expects to be on a landing craft with the first wave. He will be scared out of his mind the few minutes before the ramp goes down. But, they do it with pride and dedication. These stories are about two such brave men who wavered and lived on the edge. Well, when you live on the edge, sometimes you fall off.

The first tale is of a Marine Buck Sergeant who was on the USS YORKTOWN CVA 10 on its first cruise to the Orient after recommissioning. Any Marine who was aboard and most of the sailors remember him. He was short, dark haired and carried a "swagger stick". (A swagger stick is similar to a short cane, with metal at both ends, rarely carried by officers or noncommissioned officers.) His uniform was always perfect and so was his short crew cut.

He was overly "Gung Ho" putting men on report. This went to the extent of not only putting Marines on report, but sailors, too. I know of one second class (E5) Aerographer who was busted to third class (E4) because the sergeant (E4) put him on report for not having a cover on while in the chow line. But, one time, he overreached himself. He put a Ship Serviceman Seaman (E3) barber on report for some minor infraction.

The next time the Sergeant went for trim of his regulation hair style; he went to a barbers chair and sat down. The barber, who wore a smock, stepped aside and another barber with a smock stepped in his place. The second barber gave him a most terrible haircut. When the cocky little sergeant stood up, he turned and looked into the mirror.

He was shocked out of his mind! He began yelling and screaming dire threats to the barber who had just cut his hair. The veins in his neck bulged, his face got red as he sputtered his demands for the Name, Rank and Serial number to enable him to put the man on report. (His hair was all chopped up.) Everyone in the barber shop stopped anything they were doing. As everyone knew and despised the little sergeant, they were happy to see him so angered.

The barber pulled off his smock and his navy rank of E6 was presented to the lowly E4 sergeant! Among howls of laughter and hurrahs from the sailors in the crowded barber shop, the very irritated sergeant jammed on his cover and stomped out of the barber shop. Angry and embarrassed, with enough hate to supply the Yorktown's' steam requirements for 24 hours!

Everywhere the little Sergeant went, he was greeted with smiles from the entire crew! After that, he did not bother the sailors.

This next incident was repeated aboard other Yorktown cruises.

Down on the Enlisted men's mess deck, there was a special watertight door that opened into an area where secret weapons were kept. Nobody except authorized persons was admitted. There was a 24 hour seven days a week, armed Marine guard on that door.

Naturally, the custom was when that Marine guard was relieved; the Corporal of the Guard would briskly march in with the replacement. The ritual of Relieving the Guard was performed.

When the guard was being replaced, he was to draw his Colt .45 pistol, point it upward, drop out the magazine into his other hand, pull back the slide, thus removing any cartridge in the weapon. He then permitted it to slide forward; keeping the pistol muzzle pointed upward and then pull the trigger on the unloaded weapon. Then, he was to put the pistol back in the holster.

Now, the reader probably knows what really happened, ONE TIME. (Actually, this happened again on at least one other Yorktown cruise.)

While the Corporal of the Guard and the relief were standing there, the Marine being relieved pulled his pistol out of the holster, pulled back the slide and let it slide forward. Next, he dropped the magazine from the pistol into his other hand, pointed the pistol upward and pulled the trigger.

The roar was ear drum damaging! The powerful .45 round went out of the barrel, traveled six inches upward to the overhead that was the six inch armor plate main deck!

All hands in the mess hall took cover, the marine that was to relieve the guard ducked. The Corporal of the Guard continued to stand at attention but with a very red face. The PFC who was the guard being relieved was immediately put on report and never regained the PFC rank he lost. He lived in shame for the rest of the cruise.

The projectile was never found.

After writing these stories, I asked several former Marines about publishing them. Each Marine assured me that ok was good to do so.

After all, not ALL Marines are perfect!

THROUGH THE HATCH!

Have you ever been in a place where alcoholic refreshments are served and heard the cry, "THROUGH THE HATCH!"?

In view of the United States Marines being an old and renowned military unit, who are we to say our past Drill Instructors are wrong? That could be compared to blasphemy!

There is no doubt as long as you are in Boot Camp, the Drill Instructors are correct.

However, when you take into consideration the Marines were originally aboard ship and nautical language spoken aboard ships and the Marine descriptions of some items do not correspond, who do you believe?

In my extensive search for the truth and the roots of the two words, "DOOR" and "HATCH" I have examined the "BLUE JACKETS MANUALS" 1940 (Copyrighted in 1938, the FIRST edition), the Thirteenth edition and the Fourteenth edition. They all agree when Doors and Hatches are mentioned.

I refer to these manuals because they represent the root sources of the nautical language of our Navy, hence the Marines.

There are many types of both doors and hatches. Both may have "dogs" to make them watertight and some may not. There are watertight doors, Non- watertight doors, airtight doors and spray tight doors. (There may be "passing scuttles" in some doors through which ammunition must be passed. These are small, tube-like openings, watertight and flash proof.) However, doors are always described as in 'bulkheads", which ashore are called walls.

Hatches are different. "Hatches are horizontal openings that are used for access through decks." They may be watertight, locked down with dogs or can have covers that may have quick release hand wheels as used in Escape Hatches. However, a Hatch is the opening, not the closure on it.

The end result is that "doors" are passageways between compartments and are used in horizontal entrances or exits.

"Hatches" are located in decks or overheads. (Floors and ceilings for landlubbers.)

The next time you are in a establishment where alcohol is consumed, I am quite sure you will hear "DOWN THE HATCH! Not "THROUGH THE HATCH!"

However, in respect, you may want to call out "THROUGH THE HATCH!" in remembrance of your Drill Instructors.

Semper Fi! (But, that motto is another story.)

SEMPER FI, MAC!

Semper Fi! How often have we Marines heard that glorious phrase? It is used as a salutation and as a ending of conversations or meetings. It is said with exuberance and bravado. Have you ever wondered how it began?

During World War II, there were many slogans and sayings that implied meanings "Remember Pearl Harbor", "Loose lips sink ships" and many others. The military had their own unique sayings that meant something pertaining to their particular situations.

"Semper Fi MAC!" That saying goes back to World War II when the US Marine Amphibious Corps was making history by defeating the Japanese, one island at a time.

The draft was in full force and many reluctant young men had been brought into the Corps. Hence, there was no great love for the military, much less the Corps, which was making them into the greatest fighting men in the world. This situation brings out sarcasm in young men.

The motto of the Corps was then, as now, Semper Fidelis, but sarcastic Marines, shortened it to Semper Fi but with an, additional MAC. The whole saying was then "Semper Fi, MAC!" The word/letters MAC has been researched. The answer that keeps coming up is the first letters of"... Marine Amphibious Corps..." (Semper Fi, Mac page 137). The phrase "Semper Fi, MAC" meant "Go to HELL" (Or something of that nature.) Using this phrase generally resulted with a "Knuckle Drill "(A fist fight.) This can be viewed in the first three minutes of John Wayne's movie SANDS OF IWO JIMA.

The saying became dormant during the Korean Conflict.

It is rumored, that during the Viet Nam war, a Marines' Dad had served as a Marine during WWII. Through the Dad, the young man knew about the saying "Semper Fi, MAC". The son was then wounded. As the bandaged Marine lay in the hospital bed, a group of VIP's were being escorted through the ward by a Marine Liaison Officer. The wounded Marine was bitter because of the draft and being wounded. As the well dressed and fed VIP's passed, one spoke to him.

With all disgust, the Marine snarled "Semper Fi !!!" (Leaving off the MAC.)

The VIP turned to the liaison officer and asked "What did he mean by THAT?" The Liaison officer, either through ignorance or trying to cover up, told the VIP "Sir that is the Marines Motto. He is still PROUD to be a MARINE!"

SEMPER FI! Was adopted by the Marines of the Corps and has been an honored motto ever since.

"...I mean, that's the name of the game. You know, Semper Fi ..." (Semper Fi. . .page 368)

INCIDENTS IN THE CORPS

As a Marine, there were many instances that I recall. Most of them were a few seconds or minutes long. Not enough to write a chapter about. I shall relate a few of them. Hopefully, you will find them interesting.

It gave me a thrill when we would march Company strength with our arms and full field packs. In uniform with that many Marines, with rifles, pistols, machine guns, mortars, and esprit de Corps gave me such a good feeling of companionship. I never had that before. It gave me a great feeling. I was one of something, a force that could do well. I loved the tramp, tramp, tramp. Calling of marching cadence stirred me. That is a feeling that people do not experience do not understand.

One day in hurricane season down at the Naval Amphibious Base at Little Creek Virginia, we went to the Rifle Range at Dam Neck, Virginia to qualify with our rifles. When the buses dropped us of, it was a nice sunny day. We spent the day there. (I qualified as EXPERT with my M1 rifle.) About the time the busses were to pick us up, it began to rain. REALLY RAIN! The buses still didn't show up. We decided to march the few miles to our barracks. We put on our ponchos, turned our rifles muzzle down, buttoned up and began to march.

We immediately got very wet. Our boots were soaked in just a few minutes. As we marched from the rifle range, we got to the Navy office and barracks area. Someone began singing marching cadence. We all picked up the cadence, shoulders back, in step and marched proudly. By that time, it was REALLY raining. We looked good and sounded good. We knew that. The sailors at work and leisure opened the doors and windows and were astounded to see Marines marching and evidently happy about it! About that time, our buses showed up with our Commanding Officer aboard one of them. He told us to get in. As MARINES, we refused. He was shocked. He demanded we get on the busses. We replied, "Respectfully, sir. We will march back to the barracks!" The Major just shook his head and told the drivers to go back to the barn. But, he did not get out and join us!   That was a proud moment for our Company.

Another incident happened in California. Our company was being transported in twenty of the reliable 6X6 Dodge Trucks. The big green truck I was on was about the middle. It was a nice sunny day and the canvas was pulled forward. We were in our "greenies" with small arms. All at once, we hear yelling back by the end of the convoy. We had no idea why. Then, screaming got closer, then a few seconds later, even closer. We were very curious. What was going on? We soon found out, a red convertible with the top down pulled alongside of our truck. There was a beautiful girl driving the car. She was a blonde with a BIG smile. She would pull alongside of each truck, slow down, pull up her dress, give a big smile, wave then put her skirt down again. Then pull up to the next truck! She soon had our whole convoy yelling and screaming! What a glorious way to live! Civilians do not have experiences like that!

While at the Mare Island Marine Base, several of our companies were having a review across an open drill field. It had rained the night before and many of the marines in other companies dodged around the large puddles. Our Company Commander Major McAvoy made a comment that his company would not march around a puddle, we would march as if the puddle were not there. The other company commander said, "Ill bet you twenty bucks your company will do the same, go around the puddles!" Major McAvoy answered, "You got a BET!" As our company approached the puddles, we kept our ranks and marched through those big, deep puddles as is they were not there! Major McAvoy was very proud of us and told us the story that evening.

Major McAvoy was a good pistol shot. He had his own accurized 1911 Colt .45. He was very proud of it. He decided to have some pistol matches and compete with other companies. Nobody asked me to join the team. After all, I was a former sailor. What do sailors know about shooting! I stepped up and volunteered to be on the pistol team. At our first match, I was Top Gun and out shot the Major. He was not happy. He did not schedule another pistol match with him and me, both in the same competition. At that time, I loved my Garand M-1 rifle. I could take it apart and reassemble it….blindfolded. It served me well. At 100 yards in the prone position, I could consistently put my shots within a 1 ½ inch circle.

The Beloved Corps was good to me in many ways. I enjoyed it. Most fellow Marines could not understand why I actually liked C Rations! The esprit de Corps and the brotherhood was amazing. Actually, I had a hundred brothers in my Company! It made a man out of me.

When at a party, or at some group gathering, there are usually men who had served in the military. When in civilian clothes, we all appear the same. However, in one of the corners are the MARINES. The Brotherhood continues!

As my life continues, I am PROUD to be a MARINE. I always remember and remind others, "ONCE A MARINE, ALWAYS A MARINE!"

SEMPER FI !

Training to climb down from a ship into landing aircraft.

WOUNDED IN VIET NAM

PFC Jim T was a United States Marine; it was Sept 18, 1966 in Quang Tri Province in the Northern 1 Corps section of Vietnam. He and his fellow Marines for the last few days were in contact with elements of the 324 B North Vietnamese Regular Army outside a village called AN Dinh. At 0700 the Marines were ordered to assault that village across a 200 yard open rice paddy.

Immediately, they were under fire by mortars and machine guns.   The little feisty PFC was not happy. He was carrying a heavy load of 2,000 rounds of 7.62 ammo for the delicate M-60 machine gun. Marines called the gun "Pig". It was bad enough being part of the crew of the Pig, but to be the ammo carrier plus all the rest of the equipment he had to carry was tough. His M14 with 8 magazines of ammo for it were heavy, but when adding a cartridge belt, back pack, 4 canteens of water, it almost overwhelmed the little Marine, especially in a fecal fertilized, wet rice paddy.

The Marines were running for cover. "…you would be surprised how my little butt moved that 200 yards, we hit the raised ground firing. The barrel of the Pig got hot really fast. I burned my arm changing it…." (The Pig did not have a handle on the barrel to enable changing it safely and quickly. Gloves were issued but clumsy to carry, put on and use.)

The Marines went through some elephant grass then approached an elevated road; they stopped, using the lower nearside for a bit of cover. It was about noon, they received a command to get some rest. Some pulled some rations from their packs. One Marine lit up a pocket field stove and proceeded to heat some water in his canteen cup to make some coffee.

The sounds of more AK47s broke out. It seemed a few hundred yards ahead. The rounds began to crack overhead. The Marines were under attack from three sides! Non Commissioned officers were yelling to the new men, "KEEP YOUR HEADS DOWN!"

As Jim T. was getting as close to the ground as his Alice Gear would permit, one of the Marines behind him stood up and began to run forward. Jim yelled, "GET DOWN!" As the Marine ran past, Jim reached out to grab his ankle. He missed. The running Marine took two more steps and was hit in the chest by two AK47 rounds. He was dead when his face hit the roadway. The young Marine's blood slowly formed a dark red puddle. Fighting and dying was familiar to Jim but it still sickened him. He kept thinking, "Damn, I should have been able to grab his boot and pull him back!"

The faint sound of a mortar round being launched was heard. It seemed to be close, coming from about two hundred yards ahead. Some of the new Marines looked skyward to see the mortar round arc high above them. The older and more experienced ones ducked down and pulled their helmet closer.

The mortar round hit a tree about 20 yards to the right of Jim. There was some screaming. The Marine who was trying to boil the water for some coffee was very angry. The mortar round had sent some shrapnel into the little stove and riddled the canteen cup. The angry Marine jumped to his feet, shaking his fist and cursing the enemy who had ruined his stove, cup and the last of his coffee.

A Sergeant yelled at him to get down. Grudgingly, he slowly obeyed. He was fortunate to have, before an AK47 got him!

About then, another low "thump". Again, a mortar round was being launched. It arced to the left of Jim. It also was a bit high and hit another tree, splintering it. By this time, Jim was really hugging the ground.

WHAM! A third round hit the tree close behind Jim! The concussion drove Jim down even more into the stinking ground. A burning sensation in his shoulders and the back of his neck indicated he was hit.

Jim reached the back of his neck with his right hand, feeling something warm and wet. He quickly brought his hand in front of his face and stared at it! BLOOD! HIS BLOOD! The Marine was angry, this meant being taken to a medical unit and leaving his buddies!

The Navy Corpsman was about ten yards behind him, Jim's neck and shoulders hurt too badly to turn his head, but he yelled as loud as he could, "CORPSMAN UP! I'M HIT!"

The Corpsman yelled back, "I DON'T MAKE HOUSE CALLS!" Angrily, the wounded Marine loudly proclaimed vulgarisms about the ancestry of the Navy Corpsman. The Corpsman soon appeared, took one look at the shrapnel wounds and called for someone to get a MedEvac Chopper to get the wounded Marine out of there.

Jim was flown directly to the USS IWO JIMA LPH-2. He was rushed below decks to the ship hospital and to the Triage area.

The Triage was set up to enable the lightly wounded to be bandaged up, and sent back to duty. The more serious were sent into one of the Operating rooms. The very badly wounded, not expected to survive, were put into a holding area. Jim was laid in that holding area. He KNEW what it was and he was SCARED! He KNEW he was NOT going to surgery, he KNEW he was going to DIE, right THERE on board that Navy Ship, out in the middle of the sea! The slight, badly wounded United States Marine felt very alone.

While Marine Jim was lying on the cot, he became aware he was hit in the back of the neck and shoulders and his chest had internal sharp pains. The shrapnel punctured his neck, lungs and back. Some of the fragments entered his lungs and other parts of his chest. He was expecting frothy blood to begin to come out of his mouth. A Navy Chaplin came over and asked him if he was Catholic. Jim nodded, "Yes." The Chaplin proceeded to give the frightened young Marine Last Rites!

The Navy Chaplin completed his task and left. The scared, young Marine began to think of all the things he had done and how much he would miss going home.

Then, a Navy Corpsman with a clipboard walked up to Jim's cot and said, "You're NEXT!"

Jim gave up all hope of ever living. He was seriously wounded, had received Last Rites and now the Corpsman said he was "NEXT."

He passed out and never had the surprise of being picked up and taken to the operating room.

His next experience was loudly yelling "OUCH!" He had awakened with a bright light shining in his face and noticed people looking down at him!

"Did I DIE? WHO are these people looking down at me? Did I KNOW them when I LIVED? Am I to follow the light? Why can't I MOVE?"

A doctor had made a long, diagonal incision across his Jim's chest and was hovering over him while commanding, "Give him some more anesthesia, he is not under far enough!" (Jim still remembers that frightening moment!)

Mercifully, the young Marine went back into unconsciousness.

When the very medicated Marine woke up, he was in a soft white bed with a four inch thick mattress. Everything was clean, warm and comfortable, except for the pain in his bandaged chest, neck and back. For him, it was Heaven!

The young hero was well taken care of while on the Navy ship. Six weeks later, he was back on duty in the rotten, smelling, hot jungle.

Again, getting shot at!

This time, at Hill 55, about 10 miles SW of DaNang, he was ambling down a well worn dirt path.

PFC Jim was walking to a safe dugout to get some cigarettes. He was doing a "No! No!", walking on the crest of a hill. A puff of dirt about 10 yards in front of him caught his attention. Hmmm. Then, a few seconds later, he heard two more dirt puffs behind him jumping up! Jim realized, "I'm getting SHOT AT! A sniper is trying to KILL ME!

The trained and experienced Marine began to run down the path. Not straight ahead, but angling to the right a couple of steps and then zig to the left and then zag back to the right. He made it to his destination as fast as his short legs could carry him.

Jim did NOT want a second Purple Heart!

The running Marine's twisting, turning and his slight stature probably kept the sniper from getting a hit on Jim!

When he was in the safe dugout, resting up after his run, telling his story, he was told that 2 Marines had been killed and a few more wounded right in that spot.

A little later, Marine Sniper Carlos Hathcock and his spotter tracked and killed a sniper in that area.

(In a later year, Jim met Sgt Hathcock and thanked him for his work and service to the Beloved Corps.)

NERVOUS RESERVISTS AND WEEKEND WARRIORS

Our nation honors all the military people who keep us safe. When we see them in harms way, we see people who are putting their lives on the line for us. When a person raises their hand and swears to protect our Nation, they can be sent, at any time, to anywhere the military needs them. Regardless of whether they are "regular" or "reserves", death is final for either one of them.

Our first defenders were the Minutemen at Concord. All of the following wars have included "irregulars", reservists along with the regular military units.

Sometimes they were absorbed in the regular units and other times they fought as individual units. This applied to each branch of our military services.

At my job at General Motors, there were two Marine Reservists working with me. SSgt Robert Knight who was a combat Marine in Korea. The other was Cpl Joe South who was in Korea with the US Army. While on work breaks, we talked about many things, including the US Marines.

Both Knight and South suggested I look into the reserves. It would produce an added income along with some good outdoor activities. To a military minded person like me, it sounded good. I talked it over with my wife and she consented.

I went to the 51st Special Infantry Company office and wanted to enlist. They looked at my navy rate as PH3 and said, "What do we need with a pharmacist?" When I informed them that a PH is a Navy photographer, they welcomed me with open arms. There was an unused photo lab under a stairwell and a 4X5 Speed Graphic! They wanted me! The Marines always loved publicity!

My Marine service was during the Cuban Crisis. Every one of us in the 51st Special Infantry Company expected to be called to active duty. The only question was when. Fortunately for the Nation, the call never came. But, the obligation was there. Each and every one of we Marines trained very hard to be ready.

I served three years, until 1962, but did not reenlist. It was hinted to me that if I would reenlist, I should keep in mind that photographers were needed in a place called Viet Nam. At that time, the Marines utilized Navy photographers, Marine photographers were hard to acquire. I was especially vulnerable because my speech problem was mostly corrected by taking adult speech classes.

Two years later, General Motors promoted me to salaried Supervisor.

My life continued much better than if I would have been sent to Viet Nam!

BLUE STAR MOTHERS OF AMERICA

During World War II, there were little flags in the windows of American homes. They were not the National Flags of the United States, but small flags with red and white trim. Most of them had one or more blue stars in the white center area.

As a youngster, I saw many of those in our small town. I knew they indicated there were military men from those particular households. Also well known was that each blue star on the flag represented one person. Some of the flags had gold stars. Those indicated a death of one of the sons or daughters. However, I did not know much more about them.

Much later in life, when my son Jeffrey J. Wells, enlisted in the US Navy, I immediately purchased one of these flags and hung it in my window. That was in the year of 1990. As Jeffrey advanced in rate, I always added his new rate to the flag.

While living in Genesee County Michigan, I learned the BLUE STAR MOTHERS had originated in Flint, Michigan on February 1, 1942. At the first meeting at the Durant Hotel, 300 mothers showed up. Captain George H. Maines, had conceived the idea for this group, acted as the Chair of the first meeting. It was decided that after receiving 1,000 responses from an ad in the FLINT News Advertiser, to form a permanent organization.

On February 6th 1942, the organization was reported on Congressional record. Chapters then formed in Michigan, Ohio, Wisconsin, New York, Pennsylvania, Oregon, California, Iowa and Washington.

Nationwide, mothers volunteered throughout the tough times of World War II. They worked in hospitals, train stations, packed CARE packages to soldiers and were a working part of homeland security during times of war.

The organization not only provides support for active duty service personnel, but also promotes patriotism, assists Veterans organizations and are available to assist in homeland volunteer efforts to help our country remain strong.

As the years went by, the little flag hung in a West window of my home, it sparkled there in the bright afternoon sunlight as a remembrance of my sea faring son.

Mass Media Chief Jeffrey Wells has served 20 years in the service of our County and retired from the Navy, with the rank on Chief Petty Officer. The little Mothers flag will given to Former Chief Wells to be honorably "retired" to a suitable place of honor in his home.

CHIEF PETTY OFFICER JEFFREY J. WELLS, US NAVY

When my sole surviving son, Jeff graduated from high school, he announced to me that he would like to go to college. I asked what was his selection as a Major. He said "Photography". He then enrolled at Ferris State University and later received his degree in Television Productions. That involved still and video photography.

After graduation, his ambition was to be a US Marine photographer as I had been. Another shock, he had never mentioned the military before. I reminded him of a very bad motorcycle accident he had suffered while racing Motocross a few years prior. (He had won a trophy in the National Motocross Races.) The accident broke his nose and knee. Consequently, the knee was weak. I suggested he join the Navy. He talked with several of my friends, including Senior Chief Photographer Bruce L. Bennett (Co founder of the National

The author shanking hands with his son, Navy Chief Jeffrey J. Wells, (Ret.).

Association of Naval Photographers) and Senior Chief Photographer Victor Strickland, both suggested he enlist as a Photo Journalist.

His first assignment was aboard the USS TRIPOLI LPH 10 and was deployed to the action in Somalia. JO3 Wells video taped three fire fights incountry with the US Marines. Since then, he has served in many varied assignments aboard ships and overseas shore stations. Chief Petty Officer Wells has served 20 years and retired in 2010.

THE MARINE CORPS LEAGUE

When I became sixty five years old, looking about, my buddies were not around. They had all "gone to their reward." By having neither siblings nor close relations, there was nobody for me to pal around with. Having been active all my life in hunting, fishing, camping and other enjoyments, I had no companions (Except my wife Charlotte.)

With this in mind, a friend from fifty years ago showed up. He was Bob Knight, my Staff Sergeant with whom I served in the Beloved US Marines! After the usual greetings, he asked me if I belonged to the Marine Corps League. Up to then, I never heard of it. Bob then explained that he was the Commandant of the local Detachment and I should look into it. There were over one hundred and fifty members, and growing.

When I told him of the loss of my buddies, Bob reminded me that as a Marine, EVERY Marine was my "brother" and that I should consider the League.

At the next Detachment meeting, there was a kinship between me and the other Marines, I thought, "HERE I have ONE HUNDRED AND FIFTY BROTHERS!" I immediately signed up for a Life Membership.

My second and third favorite lifetime pastimes have been photography and shooting. (Not always in that order.) My shooting with the Flint Detachment was very good with borrowed weapons. It took awhile for me to get used to the AR15/M16. However, it was very accurate. It has no wood on it and it looked like it was made out of plastic spare parts. I began to appreciate it because of its lightweight, low recoil and noise level, but still think a 7.62 version of it would be a better combat assault rifle. As it is, it is VERY accurate. The borrowed Colt 1911 pistols were from terrible to the very best condition. There were some really well used ones and some very accurate shooters. At that time, I used what I could borrow.

After acquiring my own AR15/ M-16 and .45, my shooting began to improve quite a bit. After a few years competing with the other members of our

Detachment, I became the "Top Gun". I was firing the best scores of anyone else in the Detachment of 200 Marines with both the AR15/M16 and the 45 caliber 1911!

My AR15/M16 has a "floating barrel" and other custom work. The 1911 is a Rock River Hardball, Accurized. It is guaranteed to hold to 1 ½" inch in FIFTY YARDS! (I have no excuse for bad scores!)

I relentlessly kidded the other Marine shooters that this "Squid" scored higher than they did with both the rifle and pistol. The use of that nickname was very rarely used after that. Since then, I have always fired at least EXPERT in rifle and pistol in the annual Marine Corps League National Postal shoots. (In 2010 Annual Shoot, I received trophies for First Place High Master (Handicap Class) in each Rifle and Pistol.)

The League is a great organization. All the other military veterans organizations lose more members each year, the Marine Corps League membership continues to grow. We are the only one of the military organizations such as the Veterans of Foreign Wars, Polish League of American Veterans and the American Legion who accomplishes this.

We are a busy group of Marines (Once a Marine, Always a Marine.) who are involved in many activities. We do them with the drive and zeal Marines are noted for.

Our present Commander, Lou Bryan has taken over the Toys for Tots for two counties and has done an excellent job.

I am proud to be a Marine and my loving wife Charlotte respects me for being one of the Few, The Proud, The Marines!

Semper FI!

194

FLINT DETACHMENT #155 MARINE CORPS LEAGUE

The Detachment meets every 3rd Thursday at 7:30 PM at its new Detachment Home located at 7377 N, Dort Highway, The home is between Stanley & Mt. Morris Road on the west side of Dort Hwy. (810) 686-1879.

The Detachment is active in:
Color Guard and Honor Guard for Parades & Funerals
Toys For Tots
Young Marines Program
Annual Detachment Rifle & Pistol Matches
Annual Detachment Picnic
Annual Marine Corps Birthday Ball
Annual Golf Outing
Volunteer at VA Medical Center, Saginaw, MI
Participate in Marine Rose program (similar to Legion's Poppy Program)
Assist USMC where ever possible
USMC "Marine For Life" Program

The Detachment also has an Auxiliary if your spouse
or female relatives are interested.
Our Auxifiary provides a full meal, including drink and desert, prior to every
membership meeting (3" Thurs @6:15 PM). Cost $7.00.
Our Home is opened every Saturday between the hours of 12—5 PM

Both flags of Mt. Surabachi.

Display at the Frankenmuth, Michigan Military Museum.

Farewell.

May you have gentle breezes
and following seas.

bwana@ameritech.net